WIN FAST

SIIMON REYNOLDS is a leading expert on high performance, in business and life, with more than 50 awards for excellence to his name, and a 30-year career owning and running numerous successful companies. He co-founded the fifteenth biggest marketing services group in the world, with offices in fourteen countries.

He has won almost every major advertising award in the world, and in Australia he has won TV Commercial of the Year, Newspaper Ad of the Year, Magazine Ad of the Year and Advertising Agency of the Year, twice. His previous book, *Why People Fail*, won the silver medal at the Axiom Business Book Awards. Siimon has also won NSW Young Achiever of the Year in the career category.

Siimon now mentors entrepreneurs and CEOs from all over the world, via Skype, and has coached more than 1000 high achievers, including leading celebrities, centi-millionaires and billionaires. He has been featured on *60 Minutes*, *Today*, *Bloomberg* and many other TV programs as a high achiever, including as a Shark on Australia's original version of *Shark Tank* (*Dragon's Den*). Find out more at siimonreynolds .com.

WIN FAST

QUICK WAYS TO

ACHIEVE more,

EARN more,

and **BE** more

Siimon Reynolds

CITADEL PRESS
Kensington Publishing Corp.
www.kensingtonbooks.com

CITADEL PRESS BOOKS are published by
Kensington Publishing Corp.
119 West 40th Street
New York, NY 10018

First published by Penguin Books, 2019

All Kensington titles, imprints, and distributed lines are available at special quantity
discounts for bulk purchases for sales promotions, premiums, fund-raising,
educational, or institutional use. Special book excerpts or customized printings
can also be created to fit specific needs. For details, write or phone the office of
the Kensington sales manager: Kensington Publishing Corp., 119 West 40th
Street, New York, NY 10018, attn: Sales Department; phone 1-800-221-2647.

ISBN-13: 978-0-8065-4091-7
ISBN-10: 0-8065-4091-5

First trade paperback printing: September 2020

10 9 8 7 6 5 4 3 2 1

Printed in the United States of America

Library of Congress Control Number: 2020937435

Electronic edition:

ISBN-13: 978-0-8065-4092-4
ISBN-10: 0-8065-4092-3

For my darling Capri

CONTENTS

INTRODUCTION

The world is moving at breakneck speed.

Ambitious people like you, worldwide, are faced with a perplexing dilemma.

You know that you need to learn new and better strategies if you are to rise to a higher level, yet you have never been more pressed for time.

This stressful conundrum has been solved with *Win Fast*, a high-performance manual for the modern, time-short, success-oriented person.

Win Fast is focused on one thing and one thing only: how to improve your personal and business performance quickly. Within minutes.

Can such profound change happen so fast? Not only do I fervently believe it can, I believe most of the time that's exactly how most performance breakthroughs occur. In a moment. An instant. A second in time when suddenly a new way is realized, a decision to change is made, or knowledge is discovered that changes your whole game forever.

This book is full of such moments.

If you want to get better but you desire to do it exceedingly quickly, you have found the ultimate book.

Win Fast reveals cutting-edge techniques you can use to achieve more, earn more and be more—without having to trudge through dozens of pages to get to the gems. And without having to wait months to see results.

The world is progressing fast. If you wish to triumph, you must do the same. Armed with this how-to guide for the ultra ambitious, you'll find it far easier to be more productive and efficient. You'll learn of previously unknown tools that can transform your performance virtually instantly.

You'll also get the benefit of my thirty years' experience as a highly successful multi-award-winning entrepreneur. I have made thousands of mistakes on my path to the top. I have read more than a thousand books on personal and business high performance. I have won more than fifty business and industry awards for excellence. I have been a mentor to numerous centi-millionaires and even billionaires. In short, I have learned a lot about what it takes to succeed at the highest levels.

Win Fast is about achieving uncommon levels of success, uncommonly quickly.

I will present to you methods, procedures and systems to help you succeed in four primary arenas:

At work. What does it take to rise up the career ladder at double speed? Certainly it takes willpower and hard work, but that is not enough. The world is full of people working ungodly long hours who are not achieving their dreams.

No, you need more. You must take actions and use tactics that your competitors have not even thought of. I'll show you loads of them.

In your personal life. How can you create a level of excellence at home, with your friends and with your family? I ardently believe that to be able to call yourself a genuine success demands that you are performing superbly within your relationships, your recreation and your social life.

You'll find the methods I reveal in *Win Fast* can be applied rapidly in every area of your life where you aspire to be outstanding.

With your health. We'd all like to be healthy, but who has the time to spend ten hours in the gym every week? What you need is a series of cutting-edge strategies that can help you make major improvements in your health, energy and vitality, but that don't take mountains of time to do. I'll show you those techniques.

Inside your mind. You and I both know that trying to improve your outside circumstances without addressing the quality of your thinking is never going to work. You must simultaneously refine your mindset and your external environment. When you do, the success stars really align and you can achieve progress at startling speed.

All this I will teach you. But I require two things from you if you want to convert the wisdom in this book into tangible and remarkable results.

- You must apply what I suggest immediately. This is not a book for dabblers and dreamers. It's for committed individuals with fire in their belly for more achievement who are driven to take copious amounts of action. These techniques will undoubtedly take

you to a new, higher level, but only if you unlock their
inherent massive power by installing them as a new
operating system for your mind and body.

- You must keep an open mind. Look, some of the
concepts in this book are truly radical. It has taken me
half a lifetime to find or invent them, test them, then
refine them into their simplest possible form – so that
you can utilize them in mere minutes to improve your
life and career. But sometimes they will stretch your
understanding of what's possible.

Be assured, I will never ask you to take anything I suggest
as an inviolable truth. But I do ask you to at least try every
single technique to see for yourself how it fares in the real
world. I think you'll be stunned by the efficacy and power of
these methods to quickly transform your performance, but
only if you keep your mind open to their potential.

As the celebrated science fiction author and professor of
biochemistry Isaac Asimov put it: "Your assumptions are your
windows to the world. Scrub them off once in a while, or the
light won't come in."

Ready for the light to come in? Okay, let's get to work.

WIN FAST

USE A TIMER ALL DAY

This productivity technique is extreme,
but I use it to massively increase how
much work I get done in a day.

Here's some background to the method.

If you observe ineffective people, you will see that they make three critical productivity errors.

- First, before they start work they do not estimate how long a task will take. So they often find they don't have enough time allocated to get the job done.
- Second, they work slowly. So at the end of the day they regularly find that they haven't achieved much.
- Third, they allow people, emails and phone calls to interrupt what they're doing. So they lose concentration and often take a long time to return to the task they were working on.

Making just one of these errors is enough to greatly reduce your productivity. Doing all three of them, however, is ruinous for anybody wanting to achieve at a high level. Yet this is how most people work. So even if a person is of above-average

1

intelligence, she or he will often find their results are ordi-nary—at best.

Enter the timer method.

It's super simple, but inordinately effective. Here's how it works:

Whenever you have a task to do, first estimate how much time it's likely to take. (If it's going to take more than 90 minutes, you may wish to break the job into sections.)

Now, shorten your estimate by 20 percent.

As an example, let's say you had to write a report and you thought it would take you 60 minutes. You may give yourself only 48 minutes to do it (20 percent less than 60).

Next, find the timer on your cell phone. Set an alarm for 48 minutes and begin working on the task.

The final part of the timer method is that you do not allow any interruptions, or take a break (unless it's an emer-gency or a necessary bathroom visit). You work all the way through.

Try this method just once and you'll be amazed at how effective it is.

You are clear how much time you have. You push yourself to get the job done quickly. And you work without interrup-tions for a specific period of time. Bingo: an immediate and major increase in productivity.

The timer method works so well because it counter-acts one of the great laws of human activity, Parkinson's Law. Articulated by Cyril Northcote Parkinson, Parkin-son's Law states that "work expands so as to fill the time avail-able for its completion."

By reducing the amount of time you make available to complete a task, you work way faster. You are also very often delighted to find that by putting time pressure on yourself, you do actually get the task achieved in the limited period you gave yourself.

There's another benefit to the timer method. When you pick up the pace, you get hit with a burst of energy—you feel sharper, clearer and more motivated. It's a great feeling – certainly far better than trudging through your workload at a snail's pace.

When implementing the timer method, don't answer the phone if it rings. If someone interrupts you, tell them you'll come back to them as soon as you've finished. Working with incessant stops and starts is poisonous to effectiveness.

Yes, the technique is a little out there, and at first you may find it a tad stressful to always be monitoring your work with a timer, but within a week or so you'll get used to it and will fall in love with the awesome results it fosters.

WIN FAST ACTION STEPS

- Try using a timer for the next three consecutive work days.
- Ignore any initial discomfort about this adjustment to your routine.
- Take a moment to estimate the right amount of time you'll need, but keep it on the tight side.
- Unless it's an emergency, do not allow any interruptions to each work period.

MAKE YOUR CELL PHONE YOUR COACH

Has this ever happened to you?

You start the day all motivated and focused, then a few hours later you begin to get distracted and bogged down by events that have happened during the day.

Maybe your workload seems insurmountable. Maybe a client called you up, angry about a mistake your team made. Maybe you received one of those emails that leave you with a heavy feeling in your chest.

Whatever caused it, you were blown off track. You're no longer performing at a high level and no longer feeling good. It's a common occurrence and I know how to fix it.

Make your cell phone your coach.

Here's how you do it. Set three alarms for yourself to go off throughout the day. For the sake of example, let's make the phone beep at 11 a.m., 2 p.m. and 5 p.m.

Arrange it so that each time the phone beeps, a positive, focusing or inspirational message appears. (It's easy to do this with almost all smartphones.)

The message is up to you, but make sure whatever you

4

write brings you back on track and encourages you to perform at a higher level.

Here are some ideas for cell phone coaching messages:

"You can do this"	*"Uplift those around you"*
"Get back on track"	*"Don't forget to smile"*
"Stay cool and calm"	*"Enjoy every day"*
"Choose to be happy"	*"Pick up the pace"*
"Work quickly and smoothly"	*"Relax"*
"Be grateful"	*"Believe in yourself"*
"You're the best in the business"	*"Breathe and release your tension"*

You can use multiple coaching messages or use the same one throughout the day—the latter option works really effectively if there's a particular area of your performance or thinking you want to improve or a habit you want to eradicate.

Using your cell phone as your coach throughout the day works remarkably well. It keeps you much more focused and upbeat, all day long.

For people who feel a lot of highs and lows throughout the day, it's a game changer.

WIN FAST ACTION STEPS

- Brainstorm five motivational focus statements that really resonate with you.

- Pick the best three.
- Set your phone alarm to go off three times during the day, with a different statement each time.
- After three days, review the statements. Change and improve them as you see fit.

READ YOUR GOALS
THREE TIMES A DAY

Most people's system for achievement is incredibly haphazard, lax and ineffective.

First, most folks have no clear goals.

Sure, many of us have very general goals such as "make more money," "get fit," or the old classic, "be happy."

But if our goals are too general, they simply don't inspire action—and give us very little way to keep track of our progress.

Second, most of the people who have goals haven't written them down.

Yet research by Dr. Gail Matthews at Dominican University of California showed that having written goals increases your chances of hitting them by a massive 40 percent.

Simply writing them down makes a huge difference to your levels of achievement.

(Inversely, if you do not write down your goals, there's a real chance you'll forget you even set them.)

Third, even those who have clearly defined their goals and written them down rarely review them.

As a result, they end up forgetting them during the day, and instead get caught up in a maelstrom of urgent (yet usually unimportant) tasks.

Fast-forward a year and, typically, precious little progress has been made on their key-goals list.

These three points are why I suggest to my coaching clients a rather extreme strategy: Create clear, written goals and read them three times every day. That's right, three times. Morning, lunchtime and at the end of the work day.

Now there's not a person in 10,000 that does this, but it's a stunningly effective tactic to help you achieve at an elite level.

1. The morning read-through of your goals gets you clear, focused and motivated.
2. The midday/lunchtime goals read-through reminds you of what's important, helping you avoid getting sucked into fruitless busywork.
3. The end-of-work-day goals read-through gets you remotivated (if you've had a hard day) and reset for the next day.

This system takes only minutes, yet it will have a profound effect on your ability to think clearly, motivate yourself and determine what direction to take.

Do this for just one week and I guarantee you will not only be way more inspired, you'll also be vastly more focused in your day-to-day work. You'll reject most tasks that come up that are urgent but not important, and instead stay resolutely committed to completing more of the tasks that will actually bring you closer to your written goals.

You'll be aware, awake and focused on what counts.

Implement this system for a year and the levels of effectiveness and motivation you reach will blow your mind.

The legendary leadership expert Ken Blanchard believes that "all good performance starts with clear goals."

Reading your goals three times a day creates this ultra clarity.

WIN FAST ACTION STEPS

- Write down your goals.
- Put them somewhere that is easy and quick to access – in your phone, computer, a journal or on a card on your desk.
- Set specific times that you will take a minute to read them.
- Consider putting a reminder sticky note on your computer so that reading them becomes a habit.

PRACTICE THE TWO-HOUR DAY

*I created this technique to combat
a major problem most people
experience frequently.*

They get to the end of the day and realize that they haven't
even started on their most important tasks.

It's so easy to do. We arrive at work in the morning ready
to conquer the world, then immediately get caught up answering emails, being called into meetings or just doing the easy or
quick jobs that often don't matter much.

Pretty soon the sun is setting and the two or three crucial
tasks we hoped to do remain undone. If we're not careful, this
addiction to distraction can completely scuttle our chances of
achieving our biggest dreams.

Hence my Two-Hour Day solution.

The Two-Hour Day is a very simple method where you
pretend your work day is only two hours long.

So if you usually begin work at 9 a.m., you must do
whatever it takes to move forward on goals that really matter
to you by 11 a.m.

The key way of evaluating whether you've succeeded is

that if you had to leave work at 11 a.m., you would honestly feel that the day had already been highly productive.

Can you see how this system can empower you to profoundly improve your productivity? Imagine if by 11 a.m. each day you had got two or three seriously valuable tasks done. Wouldn't that feel amazing?

Then you have the rest of the day to either get even more crucial stuff done, or relax and do all those admin tasks or meetings that you've been putting off, knowing with confidence that you have already achieved more of genuine value than most people do in an entire day. (Or frankly, an entire week.)

To keep you focused on this method, you could even block out the first two hours of your calendar with the words "Two-Hour Day," to remind you to get moving on your imperative jobs right at the start of the day.

The trick is, you must truly act as if the day *will* end at 11 a.m. You have to work like a maniac, really pushing yourself to get things done at lightning speed. It's not enough to just focus on the crucial tasks; you must put pressure on yourself to get them done fast—by the time the clock strikes eleven.

And hey, maybe occasionally you reward yourself by actually finishing your work at 11 a.m. and taking off the rest of the day. Why not? You've already done more than most people will do by 6 p.m.

Always remember, success is based on your output, not your input. It's not the hours you work, it's the results you achieve that matter. Practice the Two-Hour Day and you will truly become a master of high achievement.

WIN FAST ACTION STEPS

- Block out the first two hours of each working day in your calendar.
- Create a list of two to four tasks that you will have completed by 11 a.m., no matter what.
- Rearrange that list in order of priority.
- As best you can, estimate how long each task will take.
- Start on one of the tasks as soon as you begin work.
- Do not start this system later than 9 a.m.

DEVELOP THE NUMBER-ONE TRAIT OF TOP-PERFORMING CEOS

One of the world's leading management researchers, Professor John Kotter of Harvard Business School, was driven by a single question.

Was there one dominant character trait that the world's most successful CEOs all shared?

To find out the answer, he and his research team studied America's top-performing CEOs, based on their companies' share-price rise over a 10-year period. They then interviewed the business titans and those who worked closely with them.

To their amazement, the researchers found that there was indeed a single characteristic that they all shared. Professor Kotter concluded that if a CEO did not have this trait, their chances of reaching the top in business were exceedingly slim. But if they did possess it, then the world was their oyster.

So what is the single most important character trait of all top-performing CEOs?

Kotter calls it "a sense of urgency."

The top performers review quickly, decide quickly and

then act quickly. They work at speeds that are far faster than ordinary people—and so they garner extraordinary results.

They push others to act quickly, too. They don't put up with long delays from the people they work with. They are constantly cajoling their staff and suppliers to get things done rapidly.

It makes sense, when you think about it. There is so much complexity in companies these days, so much inertia and red tape, that unless the person at the top is demanding speedy progress, there's every chance the company's key initiatives will get bogged down, or never even eventuate.

Corporate high-performance expert Jason Jennings puts it another way: "It's not the big that eat the small; it's the fast that eat the slow."

Now that you know Kotter's research, you need to infuse everything you do with this attitude of urgency. Insist on speed from your team, your suppliers, and importantly, from yourself.

The fact is, your team members will mimic how you yourself behave. If you live by the cult of speed, then they will, too.

Now, this does not mean that you behave recklessly. Some things take time. Some decisions need deep pondering. But the reality is that this type of decision occurs rarely. Generally, adopting an attitude of urgency is far more likely to engender success than being slow and considered.

Until recently, Mark Zuckerberg, one of the most successful company founders in history, ran Facebook by the mantra "Move fast and break things." Even now, his corporate credo is "Move fast with stable infrastructure." Note the commonality: it's critical to move fast.

So, a quick quiz for you. What's your urgency level, on a scale of one to ten?

If it's below eight you need to ramp it up. Urgently.

WIN FAST ACTION STEPS

- For one whole week, make urgency your primary goal.
- Trim the fat. Look to cut time spent on tasks, emails and meetings.
  - Demand urgency from those who work with you and for you.

The best performers focus on daily improvement, even if they've had an awesome day.

This two-question daily review can be completed in mere minutes. But it's a potent way to become a stellar performer in any field you care about.

WIN FAST ACTION STEPS

- Initially, place a reminder on your pillow to do the review.

- If you have a partner, consider doing your reviews together before you go to bed.

- If you consistently get the same answer for the "What could I have done better?" question, spend a minute or two reminding yourself of this at the start of each day to increase your resolve and focus.

CREATE A THREE-PERSON SUPERHERO

The founders of the field of psychology known as Neuro-Linguistic Programming, Richard Bandler and John Grinder, developed a fabulous way to quickly improve anyone's performance.

If you want to become good at something, just find someone who is superb at that same thing, and mimic what they do. Grinder and Bandler found that in most cases, if you think and behave like an expert in the field, you will often begin to achieve similar excellent results.

They called the technique "modeling."

Now I'd like to take their method a step further.

I want you to think of three figures who you really admire in your industry. They could be colleagues or they could be icons you've never met, but know of. They could even be deceased but known as having been the titans of your field.

Take a moment now to think of three such people.

Now write down three character traits that sum up each of these paragons of excellence. What were they like? How did they work? How did they think? In a few words, describe why they were so great.

The next step is this: if you had to combine these three masters of your industry into one personality, how would you describe it?

Sum up this awesome combo in three or four sentences or, if you're able, three single words.

Congratulations, you've just created a three-person super-hero. Your mission now is to spend all day endeavoring to behave like this hybrid person. As much as you can, attempt to act like that combination of people—in meetings, at your desk, as you think, all day long.

Think of your three-sentence summary of them often, as you go about your work.

At first it may feel a little strange, as initially you might feel you are masquerading as another personality. But stick with it. Within one week it will begin to feel more natural, and within two weeks you will definitely have started to become much more like them.

As the philosopher Ralph Waldo Emerson noted, "You become what you think about all day long."

Rather than be like the average person who is constantly worried about life and business, choose to take control of your thoughts and literally sculpt your daily thinking so that you are emulating three great people in your field.

Humans are far more malleable than we realize. We can dramatically change our personalities—through sheer will, repetition, decision and belief. Yes, it takes daily effort, but I believe the fruits are worth it.

Follow this procedure faithfully for three months and

there'll be a remarkable occurrence: your self-identity will change. You will actually see yourself as this type of person. And many of those who come into contact with you will sense the change.

People are not born great. They consciously become great, through intention and willpower, over time.

An effective way to start that process is to create your own three-person superhero and start living as this combined personality.

WIN FAST ACTION STEPS

- Give yourself just ten minutes to choose three people you really respect in your field. (You can replace people later, once you've tried the technique.)
- Remember to consider people who are no longer living.
- Once you've written your three- or four-sentence summation of their traits, read it every morning before you begin work.

CREATE A FUTURE SELF

Here's an interesting mental model that really helps people to succeed at a high level.

At the heart of the paradigm is that we all have three selves: a past-based self, a present-based self and a future self.

Our success in life depends on how much time we spend as each self.

If we spend most of our time thinking about how life was in our past—and that we are no better than our past performance—then we won't excel in the present day.

If we spend all our time living in the present, we can achieve a reasonable amount, but won't develop optimally into someone more accomplished and evolved than we already are.

But if we take the time to clearly design a better version of ourselves, then focus daily on working to become that future self, then we will always be pushing ourselves to achieve more, earn more and be more.

I love this model because it goes a long way to explain how many people fail to achieve better results over time— they are not moving consciously and deliberately towards a higher version of themselves.

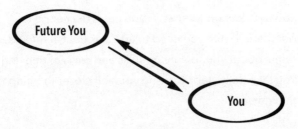

As the British philosopher James Allen put it, "Men are anxious to improve their circumstances, but are unwilling to improve themselves. They therefore remain bound."

How many people do you know who have a clear future self in their minds that each day they are methodically moving towards becoming?

Very few.

What is the ideal you? What would this future self be doing? What standards of excellence would they have reached? What character traits do you need to develop to become that person? What do you need to learn? What kind of friends does this future you have? Where do they live and what kind of clothes do they wear?

Look, in five or ten years, you are going to be a different person in some ways. Why not consciously design who that future person will be, so that when that time comes you can honestly say that you are delighted with the person who you have become?

Becoming an awesome future you depends on three key elements:

1. You get very clear on what kind of person you are going to become.

2. You get clear on what ways you need to change to get there – what you need to add, subtract, alter and refine about your behavior, skills and ways of thinking.
3. You take daily steps to bring yourself closer to being that person.

Remember, all things are created twice. First in your mind and then in action.

Getting clear on your future self and then behaving as much as possible like that person every day is the recipe to an extraordinary future life.

WIN FAST ACTION STEPS

- The trick with creating a future self is to create a trial one speedily.
- Only by "trying it on" and seeing if it feels comfortable will you get a true indication as to its suitability for your future aspirations.
- Make sure you are both inspired and excited by the thought of becoming this person.
- Once a week for a month, review your future self and look for ways to refine it, so that it's truly the optimum future You.

SPEND MORE TIME
IN FIELD FOUR

There are four fields we can spend our
daytime lives in.

How much time you spend in each field will not only dictate how much success you have in life, it will profoundly affect how much happiness you experience.

Field One is activities that you are terrible at. Even the most intelligent person has a whole slew of activities that they perform pretty badly.

Field Two is activities that you are reasonably good at, but not particularly better than a lot of other people.

Field Three is things that you are excellent at. Interestingly though, although you may be way above average at performing these tasks they may not necessarily bring you fulfillment.

Field Four is stuff that you are fabulous at and you also really enjoy. You feel energized when you do these things, and your results are far above other people's. Field Four tasks tend to come easily to you, and you wonder why other people find them difficult. All the fun for you is in this field of endeavor.

With this model in mind, I have an important question for you.

Which fields do you spend most of your time in?

Most people spend a surprisingly large amount of time in Fields One, Two and Three. Consequently, they live relatively unsuccessful and unfulfilled lives. But if you can allocate more time to Field Four, your whole life will change for the better.

In Field Four, your work will usually be of a much higher standard than that of your peers, and therefore so will your rewards. In Field Four, you will get noticed more and appreciated more. In Field Four, you will be constantly invigorated by doing what you truly love. When you think about it, a lot of the joy of life comes from living in Field Four as much as possible.

It's not always easy to increase Field Four activities, of course. Those who work for others are not completely in control of how they spend their time, and even the self-employed or at-home parents can have trouble setting aside more of their day to be in Field Four. Mundane life has a habit of getting in the way.

But try we must. Here are some tactics:

For starters, work out what your Field Four activities are. What are you excellent at that you also enjoy? It's crazy, but most people have never actually taken this first step.

Then guesstimate how many hours each week you spend on these life-enhancing Field Four activities.

Next, ask yourself how you could increase time spent in Field Four. (Just focusing on increasing it should immediately improve things.)

Finally, look at ways you could cut down on Field One and Two activities (the things you're not good at) by simply avoiding them, doing them quickly or delegating them to someone else.

Life is too short to spend much of your day doing things that you don't particularly enjoy and aren't really good at.

Once you start thinking about the Four Fields, you'll soon come up with all sorts of ways to bring more joy and success into your life.

WIN FAST ACTION STEPS

- Get clear on your Four Fields.
- In the next week, aim to spend another five hours doing Field Four actvities.
- In the next few months, slowly refine your schedule so that you are spending at least 20 hours a week in Field Four.

HAVE A CLEAR FINISH TIME

*This simple technique will massively improve both
your work and your life.*

Most people have a particular time they start work each day,
but few people are strict about what time they finish.

This often leads to executives working far later than they
should, which in turn leads to greater stress, lower levels of happiness, less exercise and poorer quality family and social life.

I recommend you be precise about what time you will
complete all your work each day, and stick to it religiously.

This one decision greatly improves both your effectiveness and your quality of life.

For a start, when you have a definite time you have to
finish work and go home, you tend to work much faster
throughout the day.

Here's an interesting example of that. Ask yourself, "What
day of the year am I at my most effective?" For most people,
the answer is the day before they go on vacation. Because you
know that you're going away, you power through all your
work, do meetings super efficiently and handle tasks at optimum speed.

If you didn't have that deadline you wouldn't have the

impetus to push yourself and others to get stuff done; you'd work at a much slower pace.

Dr Jim Loehr, the co-founder of the Human Performance Institute in Florida, conducted more than ten years of research on executive effectiveness. He found that average-performing executives made two key mistakes:

1. They didn't push themselves hard enough while at work – they worked far too slowly.
2. They didn't take enough breaks from work, working far too long most days.

His research team found that the most effective way to work is the exact opposite: work shorter hours with lots of breaks, but really push yourself to get a lot of tasks done. The result is a greater output and greater total rest per day. A fabulous combination, I'm sure you'll agree.

Having a clear finish time makes you both a faster worker and a more relaxed one. It also sets the stage for having an enviably balanced life.

Always remember that to be ultra successful, your primary focus needs to be your results, not time and effort. The two are not always correlated. Unfortunately, many of us have been indoctrinated by the traditional corporate culture where time spent at the desk is viewed as most important, rather than quality and quantity of output. That's a crazy situation that leads to millions of workers being too scared to leave their workplace until it's dark outside, for fear of giving an impression of laziness or low commitment.

We must develop the courage to be obsessively results focused, not time and effort focused. And having a definite finish time is an excellent way to achieve that.

WIN FAST ACTION STEPS

- Pick your finish time.
- Tell those around you that you will finish by then no matter what, explain why and ask for their support.
- Put "Finish right now" at that time, Monday to Friday, in your calendar.
- If you have difficulty adhering to the finish time, insert a warning in your diary halfway through the day and 30 minutes before your finish time.

HAVE A MACRO TO-DO LIST

There's no doubt that writing a To-Do list improves how much you get done in a day, week or year.

But there are two key problems with the typical To-Do list.

Either it usually has so many tasks on it that it's absolutely impossible to finish them or even figure out what to do next, or it's not truly comprehensive—it has numerous To-Do's left off it, so it can't really be trusted as a true record of what you have to do.

Either situation makes a To-Do list ineffective.

After years of studying time management and self-organization, I've found the solution to this problem. I call it the Macro To-Do list.

The Macro To-Do list is a giant list of every single task you have to do in your life, both business and personal. Any time you think of anything you need to do, you put it on the Macro To-Do list—even if you can't foresee when you will be able to do it.

Then every few days you simply spend a few minutes reviewing the list—keeping it organized and up-to-date.

But it is very important that you not use this list as your Daily To-Do list.

You have a second list for that. Your new Daily To-Do list is short. It's just the handful of tasks you really have to get done that day (business and personal).

Having both a Macro To-Do list and a short Daily To-Do list makes a colossal difference to both your efficiency and your stress levels.

You Daily To-Do list is now simple, clear and focused. And importantly, it is an accurate list of what you need to do that very day. It's not a mountain of tasks of every description that you could never possibly get done in 24 hours (or frankly, even a week). It has a Zen minimalist quality to it. It's just the essential tasks that need completing for the day to go well.

The Macro To-Do list will calm you enormously. Because from now on, all the tasks that you ever need to carry out will be recorded on this big list, so you know you'll never forget them. You'll visit the big list every day or two, reviewing and organizing a complete inventory of tasks you need to complete.

This is tremendously stress relieving, as you'll never again have that sinking feeling of knowing there is something you have to do, but not being able to remember what it is. Everything will be safely recorded on your Macro To-Do list.

At the heart of this marvelous organization method is a major change of habit. From now on you must write everything you need to do down on paper, not keep it in your head. It's when you try to remember lots of tasks that you inevitably end up forgetting things, missing deadlines and getting stressed.

So try the Macro To-Do list and the simplified Daily To-Do list. They're a godsend for any ambitious person.

WIN FAST ACTION STEPS

- Allocate 15 minutes right now to creating your first Macro To-Do list.
- Rewrite today's To-Do list, making sure you have fewer than ten items on it, until you get used to working this way.
- Treat your Daily To-Do list with a new attitude. Only put what you will absolutely get done on it.

LIVE BY THE 64/4 RULE

One of the most powerful rules in the universe is surely the 80/20 Principle.

First posited by the Italian economist Vilfredo Pareto in the nineteenth century, it states that roughly "20 percent of what you do gives you 80 percent of your results."

Oh what magic stems from those fifteen words! Live by them and you can be one of the greatest achievers of our time. Fail to live by them and you are destined to compete at a similar level to everyone else.

That's because most people work by an opposite principle—that you can only *get* more by *doing* more. Pareto said that's hogwash. He fervently believed that most of what we do has very little impact on our results, and therefore you don't have to do more to achieve more, you could actually do a whole lot less and achieve more. As long as what you did was part of the 20 percent of your activities that are really valuable.

This has huge ramifications for your life. It suggests that you should be very, very careful about what you choose to do. It suggests that if you chose your activities more wisely, you

4 = 64

could work only a few hours a day and achieve much more than you do currently.

It opens the possibility that you do not in fact have a shortage of time, as most people believe. You actually have huge amounts of time, if only you utilized it properly, in accordance with the 80/20 Principle.

So if the 80/20 Principle is so life changing, what is the 64/4 Rule?

Well, if you can win faster by doing more of the most vital 20 percent of your activities, what if you went one step further? What if you focused on the most important 20 percent of that important 20 percent?

Then you would find that a tiny 4 percent of what you do accounts for 64 percent of all your results. Just think of the implications of this! If these principles hold true, and many who've lived by them believe that they do, then you could achieve colossal amounts in your life by focusing on just 4 percent of your current activities. Or you could potentially take your life to an entirely new level by choosing to focus on the crucial 4 percent of an entirely different set of activities. Truly the tiniest of actions could well lead to stupendous results.

That is the highly enticing premise of the 64/4 Rule.

But it should not just remain as an abstract construct for you. You must put it to the test.

Spend ten minutes thinking about all the activities that you do at work. Which of these yield most of the good results? That's the 20 percent of the 80/20 Principle. Now think about which of those activities that comprise the 20 percent are much more useful than the others from this section? These are the 4 percent in the 64/4 Rule.

Once you've determined what the most valuable of the worthwhile 20 percent of actions are, you must now spend as much time as you can on carrying out more of that 4 percent.

Imagine for a moment if you could spend twice as much time each week on the 4 percent of activities that bring you 64 percent of results. That would lead to an absolutely vast improvement in what you achieve in life.

You wouldn't be working any harder, you could in fact be working far less. But your results would go through the roof.

WIN FAST ACTION STEPS

- Work out your top three most valuable work tasks.
- Decide the top three most important activities in your personal life.
- Aim to spend double the time on each of these six areas.

FAST ONE DAY A WEEK

*For centuries, fasting has been seen as a way
to dramatically improve someone's health and
mindset.*

But lately, researchers have discovered just how effective it can
be as a performance enhancer.

According to multiple studies done on intermittent fasting, when you take a break from food for 16–24 hours, some
pretty impressive changes happen to your body.

- Human growth hormone, your body's
  own wonder drug, increases substantially,
  helping to boost muscle growth, strength
  and exercise performance, while helping you
  recover from injury and disease.
- You experience improved cognitive function
  such as mental flexibility, and higher
  parasympathetic activity in the brain, which
  acts like a brake, calming the body with
  effects that include conservation of energy
  and more efficient digestion. (Although many

people envisage a loss of mental focus during
a fast, many people report that they actually
start thinking more clearly than usual.)

- You boost metabolism, which can enhance
weight loss. (After 13-16 hours, your body
switches from burning glycogen to fat
burning.) Fasting may improve blood-sugar
control, too, helping you to avoid the lethargy
and hunger that comes from blood-sugar
spikes.
- You can protect against immune system
damage and induce immune system
regeneration, shifting cells from a dormant
state to a state of renewal.

Pretty amazing results, don't you think?

The fact is that regular fasting is one of the very best tactics you can do to keep yourself healthy.

And to help you live longer. According to many gerontologists, reducing calories is one of the surest ways to increase the likelihood of a long life. For example, tests on many mammals have shown substantially enhanced lifespan with calorie deprivation. Research on humans, while not as conclusive, certainly points to a similar potential result.

I first learned about the power of fasting when I was writing a book on longevity many years ago. And today I fast all day until dinner, Monday to Friday each week.

You don't have to be as extreme, of course. You'll still give yourself the chance to get some fantastic health advantages with much smaller breaks from eating.

The three most popular fasts currently are:

1. Fasting for 16 hours daily, one day a week. This usually means having dinner then not eating until around noon. Pretty easy to do for most people.
2. The famous 5:2 Diet. In essence, this consists of five days a week eating regularly and two days (not in a row) of consuming only around 500 calories.
3. Going 24 hours without food, several times a year.

Each method has its evangelists, all of them have good research to support them and they are each simple to follow.

The food part is easy to understand, but what about liquids?

Well, there are many points of view on this. Some experts recommend that you consume juices throughout the day. Others suggest you achieve a better result by only drinking water or tea. The one aspect they are in agreement on is that you must consume plenty of liquid during any fast that you do. Reducing hydration while fasting is potentially very dangerous.

Fasting may sound strange at first, and it certainly takes some getting used to, but once you've done it a few times you may well become a fan.

Less fat. More energy. Clearer thinking. And potentially a longer life. Many think people who fast are crazy, but I think you'd be crazy not to.

WIN FAST ACTION STEPS

- Pick a day this week that you will attempt your first fast.
- Make sure you have a substantial and nutritious meal the night before.
- Only give up that first trial if you are feeling weak or sick, otherwise just keep powering through.
- Drink plenty of water, tea or some coffee through the day.
- Take note of any positive mental changes you experience, such as increased focus, calm or optimism.

WORK UNDER FULL-SPECTRUM LIGHTING

Everyone knows that natural sunlight is beneficial to health.

But almost nobody is aware that you can buy light bulbs that mimic many of the benefits of being in the sun.

In fact, this special type of light bulb improves almost every aspect of your work life.

This bulb is called full-spectrum lighting and its advantages are numerous.

Like the name suggests, full-spectrum lights give out all seven colors of the rainbow, not just white, like most standard light bulbs.

This makes working in your office feel much more like you are working outdoors in daylight. Rather than putting up with the intensity of fluorescent lighting, you can enjoy a much warmer, invigorating style of light.

The sights around you will definitely look better, but most of the benefits of full-spectrum lighting (FSL) occur inside you.

Research indicates FSL greatly improves your general mood. It's actually used as a therapy for those with seasonal affective disorder.

It also helps your body synthesize vitamin D, so you receive more of its benefits, including bone health (low levels of vitamin D have been linked to diseases such as osteoporosis). Those who live in areas with fewer daylight hours are more likely to have some specific cancers (colon, ovarian, pancreatic and prostate), and the World Health Organization advises that exposure to daylight may help treat skin conditions such as psoriasis, eczema, jaundice and acne.

Using full-spectrum lighting can improve productivity, too, by making you more alert and increasing your ability to concentrate for longer.

But the benefits don't stop there. Some studies show it improves your sleep patterns, as your body clock (or circadian rhythm) is closely linked to the intensity, timing and duration of shorter wavelengths that are in the full spectrum.

So with all these high-performance benefits, why doesn't everyone use full-spectrum lighting?

Well for starters, the vast majority of people are simply not aware of its existence. FSL light bulbs are also more expensive than conventional ones. Moreover, it's not always easy to find this kind of light bulb in stores, though that is slowly changing—for example, GE, one of North America's major light bulb suppliers, now sells their FSL light bulbs in many pharmacies. They are easy to purchase online, however.

But these are minor inconveniences compared to the compelling advantages of using full-spectrum lighting. Anybody who wants to improve their health and performance should seriously consider this alternative lighting source.

WIN FAST ACTION STEPS

- Go online and research full-spectrum lighting.
- Buy one or two bulbs and try them in one room at first – the office is ideal.
- After one week, if you experience a positive difference, look at using these lights in other rooms in your environment.

TO DOMINATE MEETINGS, ASK QUESTIONS

Doing meetings well is both an art and a science.

It's an art because it involves intuition and empathy—you need to intuit the meaning and true intent and desires that exist behind what people are saying. Their words are just a small portion of the total data you need to analyze.

It's a science because there are some specific techniques you can use that will dramatically increase your success whenever you meet with people.

I'm going to teach you one method that I've developed and enhanced over the years that can help you get optimized results in any meeting.

It's built around asking questions. I've observed that the person who dominates and makes the biggest impression in a meeting is almost always the person who asks the most questions. So if you want to shine in a meeting, if you want to get noticed or establish your seniority and exhibit more power, then you need to ask a lot of questions.

Here's why it's so effective.

The person who asks the most questions controls the

meeting. People are either looking at the one who is doing the asking or responding to what they said. Consequently, the center of the meeting becomes the question asker.

It's almost impossible to make a wrong step asking questions. It's a whole lot easier to ask intelligent questions than to give intelligent answers! You apply pressure on others and avoid it yourself.

Questions are easy to prepare prior to the meeting. Done well, they can make you look brilliant. (People often assume somebody asking a smart question must be wise. That is often not the case—perhaps they just prepared well before the meeting.)

To fully appreciate the advantages of asking the most questions, consider the inverse. What type of impression does someone who is quiet in a meeting give off?

Much of the time they look as though they are less powerful, less impactful, less involved and less cognizant of the issues being discussed.

(The exception to this is when someone known to everybody in the room as the boss is silent. Their power is already firmly established, so silence can work well for them.)

Here are some tips for dominating meetings with questions.

Prepare your questions well before the meeting. Ten or twenty minutes brainstorming a series of perceptive questions a day before the meet-up is scheduled is time very well spent.

Also allocate some time to think through different directions the meeting may head in. You might create some lists for each. If you think the meeting could go in one direction, design some questions around that. If it could head in another direction, you prepare a few questions for that eventuality.

Always have a few provocative questions up your sleeve. But make sure you deliver them with a warm and friendly tone of voice.

One last tip. If you have no idea what to say in a meeting and you're in danger of being a minor player, you can exert instant control by asking some general "more information please" questions.

Like the following: "Why do you think that?" "Is there any data to support that?" "Can you go a little deeper with that thought?" "What's your level of confidence that this is going to happen?" "That's interesting. Can you tell me more about that?" "Well, what would you suggest to fix that?"

These are easy to ask but can really make an impact in a meeting and greatly enhance your status in it. If you want to dominate meetings, questions are the answer. No question.

WIN FAST ACTION STEPS

- One of the best tools you can have in business and life is a series of memorized questions that you can use in any conversation, which can make you look good, get people to open up and help to build trust with others. Using the examples above as thought-starters, write a few of your own that you feel comfortable asking regularly.

- Now commit them to memory, then use them as soon as you can in some conversations over the next few days.

FOLLOW THE 80 PERCENT GOOD PRINCIPLE

Society admires perfectionists.

The author who slaves for eight years to produce a book. The entrepreneur who works 18 hours a day, seven days a week, to build her company. The ballet dancer who practices one movement so much that he dreams of it in his sleep.

And certainly, there is much to admire in their obsessive and relentless action.

But I think that most of the time, perfectionism actually reduces your chances of success, not increases it.

Not only do most tasks not have to be done perfectly, but wasting hours of extra time working on these things until they are perfect is usually a really bad use of your time.

I would argue that for most people in most situations, perfectionism actually leads to mediocrity.

In most cases, you would be much better off if you just finished tasks quickly and moved on to getting another one done.

I'm not talking about doing shoddy work; far from it. I'm talking about doing things 80 percent of the way to perfect, then moving on and getting something else done.

FOLLOW MY FOUR-STEP PRODUCTIVITY SYSTEM

There have been thousands of books written on productivity, many of them contradicting the others. Working out which advice to take can be overwhelming.

Let me save you from any confusion. Just follow the Four-Step Productivity System below. This simple yet powerful method has helped me (and my coaching clients) massively increase their success and reduce their stress.

The system is based around what you allow on your computer screen.

That's because there's one thing almost everyone does that generally halves their rate of daily achievement: leaving their email open on their computer screen all day.

This single act has a stupendously bad effect on your productivity, in two insidious ways.

It breaks your concentration constantly, because as new emails arrive, you notice them and often stop what you are doing to address them.

And it makes you focus on other people's priorities—their email requests—instead of your own goals.

Both of these outcomes are extremely deleterious to your performance.

There is simply no way you can achieve at an optimum level if your concentration is being endlessly broken by seeing new emails coming in to your inbox.

The temptation to read them is enormous. Very few people have the iron will needed to ignore a juicy, intriguing email when it pops onto your screen. Some of them *are* just irresistible!

No, the only method that I've found works is to prevent yourself from seeing the emails in the first place.

You've got to hide them from yourself—and that means you need to make sure that they are not the default that you see on your computer screen every time you look up from your desk.

That change alone will dramatically increase your daily productivity. You won't be distracted by new emails and you won't lose time reading and answering some of them. A double win.

But to really maximize your achievement, we need to go two steps further.

First, you need to replace the email screen with your computer's calendar screen (the page that outlines what appointments you have each week).

And second, you have to fill your day's calendar with your Daily To-Do list. I want you to literally plan your whole day and allocate time on your calendar for each major task.

When you do both these things, your effectiveness will skyrocket.

All day long you'll be looking at your To-Do list on your calendar, not your emails. It will make you much more time sensitive, as you'll see that you must finish your current task quickly, because a new one is scheduled to start soon.

This system will create the all-important urgency mentioned earlier in the book.

And by inputting to your computer's calendar the clear periods of your day that you will get your most important jobs done, you are much more likely to achieve them.

Here's the reality: most people let themselves be interrupted by emails all day. Most people don't even have a To-Do list. And even those who have such a list usually don't allocate clear times in their day to get these tasks done.

Result? Mediocre performance and ordinary results.

By making these three easy but vital changes, your productivity will improve hugely.

Which only leaves one question: When do you look at your emails?

Well, the fourth step in my Four-Step Productivity System is to only look at your emails three times per day. Start by doing an email session first thing in the morning. Then do one around lunchtime and one at the end of the day. Between 15 and 30 minutes for each session should be sufficient.

Dealing with emails in three blocks is the fourth step that will stop emailing from taking over your life and often double your productivity.

This is my Four-Step Productivity System. Try it for two weeks and watch your productivity soar.

WIN FAST ACTION STEPS

- Put your computer's daily calendar on your screen as the default, never your email.
  - Input the key tasks from your daily To-Do list into that day's calendar so you can see what you have to do and when.
- Do emails at only three times of the day. At the start, around lunchtime, and near the end of the day.

DON'T ANSWER THE PHONE 90 PERCENT OF THE TIME

Modern slavery was abolished around the mid-nineteenth century.

So why are you still a slave?

You're not alone. Billions of people around the world are currently happily living as slaves.

To their cell phones.

Am I exaggerating? Well, let's look at your situation. Is it not true that whenever someone calls you on your phone, in almost all cases you answer it? The phone commands and you obey. The phone pays you nothing and makes you do what it says, seven days a week. Hey, call it what you want, but that looks a whole lot like slavery to me.

You need to stop this. It's ruining your effectiveness and putting up a giant roadblock between you and your dreams.

Answering your phone hurts you in several ways. First, it reduces the time you spend working on your goals. Presumably, when you are hard at work you are trying to improve your life situation. The more calls you take while undertaking this important work, usually the less progress you will make.

Answering the phone also makes it very hard to refocus on what you were working on prior to the phone's interruption. No doubt you've heard about the research that shows that every time you get interrupted it can take between ten and twenty minutes for your mind to return to its original focused state. Over the course of a year, that amounts to many dozens of hours lost to phone interruptions.

Now, I'm not naive. I know that there are some calls you really must take during your work day: either those that are very important to moving your goals forward, or emergencies. But these kinds of calls are not frequent. Usually the caller is trying to move their own goals forward, not yours.

But I would argue that even in the case where the call looks useful, in most cases you should not answer it there and then. You should design your day so that you return all your calls in blocks, twice a day. Mid-morning and near the end of the day are ideal times. That way you can batch all your missed calls together and call people back one after another. This will majorly increase your efficiency.

You need to start putting yourself first, not the agendas of other people.

Not answering the phone 90 percent of the time and returning calls twice during the day allows you to do that.

WIN FAST ACTION STEPS

- Turn off your cell phone most of the day, so you are not tempted to take incoming calls.

- Set up two blocks of thirty minutes in your calendar, Monday to Friday, to enable you to return calls one after another.

- Consider changing your voicemail message to explain this is how you work and that you'll get back to callers soon. Consider also saying on the voicemail that you prefer callers to email you, unless it's a major issue where discussion is needed.

HAVE A LEARNING GOAL
EACH QUARTER

People have a love/hate relationship
with setting goals.

They know they should set them to be more focused and productive. Yet, at the same time, many folks have set so many goals and not followed through with them that the very act of goal setting makes them feel sick.

Eventually many people decide, consciously or subconsciously, not to set any goals at all, merely to avoid the emptiness that accompanies not reaching them.

The answer is surely not to avoid setting goals, but to get really good at achieving them.

And there's one very powerful way to at least triple your chances of achieving any major goal you want to crush.

Here's how it works.

When you next set a goal, don't just think of the outcome and the steps needed to accomplish it. Also ask yourself, "Who would I need to *become* to reach this goal?"

Very few of us do this. An executive may set the goal of becoming the CEO of a company, for example, then decide that the steps to achieving it are to: work ten hours more a week, improve relationships with those above them in the company and win three new clients for the firm.

Each one of these aims may be valid and may indeed help them, but ultimately to achieve big goals we usually need to become someone greater. As the famous executive coach Marshall Goldsmith puts it, "What got you here won't get you there."

So think of a goal that you are currently shooting for. What type of person could achieve this goal? What would their character traits be? Would they need to be highly confident, more empathetic, super efficient or more creative?

Now ask yourself which of these traits do you currently possess and which you will need to develop.

Finally, ask yourself which traits you have that you would need to *eradicate* to achieve this cherished goal. What kind of person should you stop being?

Once you've collated the list of traits required and traits that must be jettisoned, pick the two most important and start focusing on becoming that person. It will make a huge difference in how may goals you achieve.

WIN FAST ACTION STEPS

- Separate your goals into five categories: health, career/finance, relationships, spiritual and social.
- Write down two traits you would need to develop to excel in each of these areas.

BECOME A MASTER OF
THANK-YOU NOTES

Want to make a huge impact on a lot of important people?

Want to be remembered for decades after you meet somebody?

Want people to think so highly of you that they talk about you in glowing terms to others?

You can achieve all this if you just start doing one tiny, easy, inexpensive activity.

Write thank-you notes.

Remember that I did not say "email thank-you notes"; I said write them.

With a pen and some beautiful paper and an envelope.

In today's frantically paced, digital-obsessed world, receiving a handwritten, thoughtful thank-you note is a total rarity. Hence it makes a hell of an impact.

I know people who have kept thank-you notes for decades! I know someone who has a thank-you note they once received stuck to their fridge. You have probably seen executives who have framed treasured thank-you notes to display prominently in their office.

Think about this phenomenon for a minute. Someone

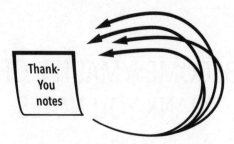

The effects of thank-you notes keep coming back

takes a few minutes to write a few words and then often gets remembered for a lifetime. Why? How on earth does this happen?

Several reasons.

A handwritten note stands out a mile from the thousands of emails.

It says that you respect the recipient and care enough about them to take the time out of your own busy day to express your gratitude.

It says that you are not like everyone else—you have class, panache and an ample dose of human decency.

It says you are a cut above the masses. Someone to remember for the future.

The humble thank-you note is one of the most underestimated techniques of all time to make a positive impact on someone you value.

Yet weirdly, ridiculously, it is hardly ever sent.

When was the last time you received a handwritten thank-you note? Maybe years ago. Maybe never. Their rarity is your opportunity.

Go and buy a pack of beautifully designed thank-you cards and envelopes.

Then at the end of every week, take 20 minutes to hand write at least one thank-you note to someone. Maybe it's a friend you really appreciate. Maybe it's a client who has trusted you with their business. Perhaps it's to an employee or workmate who has done a fine job.

Get in the habit of doing this and in a year's time you will have touched the heart of more than 50 people who matter to you.

Do this for life and you will utterly transform your relationships with more than a thousand people.

Then watch how your act of chivalry comes back to you, in the guise of deeper friendships, more business deals, more money and more people recommending you to others.

As the classic Chinese text the *Tao Te Ching* has it, "The heart that gives gathers."

Separate from any benefit you may gain from writing such notes, arguably the greatest benefit of this almost forgotten method is how it makes you feel inside.

In a word, fabulous.

WIN FAST ACTION STEPS

- Order some nice thank-you stationery, envelopes and at least 100 stamps.

- Write the first five thank-yous quickly, to embed it as a new good habit.
- Keep the stationery where you see it often, as a reminder to send more.

GO SUPER ON FISH OIL

Every year more research comes out showing that consuming fish oil has the potential to hugely improve a human's performance, in a variety of important ways.

Fish oil is essential for brain function and has been shown in numerous clinical studies to make you think and feel better, primarily due to the fact that fish oil contains two types of omega-3 fatty acids.

Want to have a higher IQ? Taking fish oil can help with learning and memory.

Need to be more creative? Fish oil has been shown to improve blood flow to the brain, reducing mental fatigue and reaction times.

Feeling a bit down? Taking fish-oil supplements can improve depressive symptoms.

The more you look into the research on fish oil, the more you'll conclude that fish oil is Mother Nature's wonder drug. I'm amazed at how powerful it can be.

There are only two problems with fish oil. Most people don't take enough of it, and much of the fish oil sold in stores is not pharmaceutical grade and therefore not that effective.

Not that the standard versions won't still be beneficial, but many of the most spectacular reported results occurred when the fish oils used were premium grade and when the doses were large.

There have been some extreme and amazing examples of humans benefiting from pharmaceutical-grade fish oil. For instance, Dr Barry Sears, an esteemed biochemist, has seen patients with advanced dementia brought back from a virtual zombie state with high doses of fish oil.

Kids with severe ADHD have seen remarkable improvements in attention, impulsiveness and cooperation within short periods of time with omega-3 supplementation. There are even studies where some colon, prostate and breast cancer patients responded stunningly well to fish oil—but once again only when major amounts of it were consumed.

In some of these studies, the dosage consumed each day was massive, and in several cases, more than 20,000 milligrams per day.

Now, however fascinating such studies are, I'm definitely not suggesting you take anywhere near that level of fish oil.

You should consult a medical professional for advice on how many milligrams per day you could consider taking. The pills may look large, but don't fret, they are not too difficult to swallow.

One question I'm regularly asked is, "Can't you get the same amount of fish oil just by eating fish?"

I wish. No, to consume the same amount of fish oil from fish you'd have to eat dozens of them a day!

So supplementation really is the only way.

Taking high-quality fish oil can make you smarter, happier and healthier.

From improved eye, bone and joint health to reduced inflammation and fat in your liver, fish oil really is one of the greatest performance enhancers you can get. So get it.

WIN FAST ACTION STEPS

- Spend 15 minutes reviewing fish-oil brands online.
  - Make a decision right away and purchase the highest grade within your budget.
- Consider subscribing to a monthly fish-oil delivery, so you'll always have a ready supply.

USE THE RELEASE BREATH TO KEEP YOUR STRESS LOW

High stress is a close companion of many high-achieving individuals. It's so prevalent that many of us just accept it as the way modern life is.

I totally disagree with that notion.

It doesn't matter how busy you are, there are numerous highly efficient methods of reducing stress to low levels.

For example, the head of the world's largest hedge fund, Ray Dalio, has been doing Transcendental Meditation (TM) daily to keep his stress low since the 1970s. Leadership expert Robin Sharma has two massages a week to keep his stress at bay. Some top achievers even visit a hypnotist to reduce their anxiety. The available options for stress relief are plentiful and varied.

But if you don't have the patience for meditation and you don't feel like forking out the money to get massages every few days, I have a solution I think you'll really like.

I call it the release breath.

I based my technique on the original work of Lester Levinson. In the early 1980s, Lester was a successful businessman who found himself sick, stressed and miserable. But unlike most in this predicament, he analysed his situation, did copious amounts of research and developed a system to slowly bring himself back to health.

His system, called the Sedona Method and still practiced today, was based on a simple but profound observation:

There are two common ways people handle their stress. They either bottle it up inside themselves, or they express it to someone involved in the situation.

Both have disadvantages. Keeping it inside you means the stress can build up to a terrible degree, and expressing it to someone may get it off your chest, but it can also create further problems, sometimes worse than the original cause of the stress.

But wise old Lester realized there was a third option: systematically reduce your stress throughout the day by releasing it. That way it never gets to rise to a high level.

When I first heard the concept, I thought it was astoundingly simple but brilliant. It makes so much sense that if we are regularly releasing our stress during the day, by the end of the day, week or month our stress level will have been kept in check and probably remain low.

Although many people swear by the Sedona Method, the challenge I had was that I didn't find his system for reducing stress throughout the day helped me that much.

So I invented my own. I call it the release breath.

With the release breath, whenever a stressful event happens, or you are thinking stressful thoughts, you simply take one deep breath and then exhale forcefully, imagining the stress immediately leaving you.

By linking stress relief with breath release, I found it greatly increased how much better I felt than when following Lester's method.

The release breath is easy to test. Just think for a moment about your current stress level, ranking it with a number out of ten. For example, three out of ten is very low stress, whereas eight out of ten would be highly stressed. Then think about what is stressing you, take a big breath in, then forcefully exhale as you imagine the stress leaving your body.

Finally, on a scale of one to ten, reevaluate what your stress level is now. I bet it's gone down considerably.

Whenever something happens that makes you stressed over the next day, deploy the release breath between three and ten times. I am confident that you'll find your stress levels will dissipate to at least half what they used to be.

In fact I'm highly confident that if you practice the release breath each day, your stress levels will never be the same again. This unusual technique is unusually effective.

WIN FAST ACTION STEPS

- If you find the release breath effective, speak to your workmates, partner or family about them trying it, too. It will change your life enormously if key people around you are also using this technique.

GET AN ACCOUNTABILITY PARTNER

No matter how successful we are, we are all human. At times we get lazy, we give up on our cherished goals, we perform at a lower level than we aspired to reach.

One of the main reasons we get away with doing this is because often nobody else is watching and evaluating our performance. Many of our personal aims and goals we keep to ourselves, so when it looks like we aren't going to achieve them, there is no one around to keep us on track, encourage us and push us to actually deliver on what we sought to do.

That's why I highly recommend getting an accountability partner.

An accountability partner is simply someone you have to report back to regularly on your progress. They could be a friend you respect, an associate with experience in your field, or even a professional business coach. Whomever you choose, both of you need to commit to a meeting or phone call at regular intervals, with the primary topic being whether you did what you promised you would do the last time you spoke.

For many people, having an accountability partner was the single most important step they took to turning their business (and often life) around.

The fact is we all get better when somebody's watching.

In the 1920s, there was a remarkable research study that reflects this phenomenon, which came to be known as the Hawthorne Effect.

Researchers were brought in to the Western Electric Company to see if they could improve the workers' performance. They came up with a series of changes for employees to make that could potentially improve results.

But then a very strange thing happened.

With every single change the researchers made, the employees' performance improved. If they changed the lighting, the employees' productivity increased. If they adjusted the temperature, the employees' effectiveness also got better. Every test they did resulted in an enhancement in output by the workers.

The head of the factory thought deeply about this remarkable result. The researchers were either geniuses or there was another element involved.

Eventually they worked out the reason. The employees' performance improved for one primary reason: Someone was observing them! Because they were being watched, they put more care and effort into what they did.

And the study became famous in management circles.

Accountability lifts everybody's performance, in any field.

If you are dedicated to being the best in your area of expertise, you must get someone to keep you at your best, stretch you and cajole you to improve in the areas that matter most to you. You need an accountability partner.

How do you set up an accountability relationship?

Just reach out to someone who you feel would work well as an accountability partner. Once you have their agreement, decide how often you will talk (every week or every two weeks works well; some even have a daily call, but that is pretty rare). Then lock these times in your calendar.

Here's how to undertake the actual accountability process: Make sure each call has the same format. For example, the call duration is always the same (10–20 minutes should be fine). You may even create a series of standard questions your accountability partner asks you. For a fascinating example of this, google "Marshall Goldsmith questions" and see what questions Goldsmith, one of the world's most respected leadership coaches, gets his accountability partner to ask him at the end of each day.

Typical areas you can be kept accountable on include: what work tasks you'll get done before the next accountability call; what type of person you aspire to be; how much you'll exercise; what new skills you'll learn; who you'll reach out to; and what problems you will fix.

The truth is, any arena you want to get better in is ripe for increased accountability. Having an accountability partner is a stunningly effective technique to maximize your greatness.

WIN FAST ACTION STEPS

- Think of three people who would make a good accountability partner.
- Rank them in order of whom you'd most prefer.
- Reach out to person number one and sell them on the benefits of being your partner.
- Set a 30-day trial period, at the end of which both parties review whether they see value in continuing.
- Be sure to schedule and stick to clear times when you will talk with your accountability partner.

TRAIN YOUR
SELF-CONTROL DAILY

We live in a world of instant gratification. Never in history has it been so easy and so quick to obtain so much.

Our ancestors had to hunt for hours just to get something for dinner. We just open the fridge.

Once it took days to travel interstate. Now we do it in hours.

In the old days people had to wait all week for their favorite shows to appear on TV. Now you just click a few buttons and there they are.

While this is generally marvelous, in one way it's quite disastrous. We are losing the self-discipline of waiting.

This may not seem like much but I can assure you it is a very big deal.

Because self-control—the ability to defer immediate pleasure in order to enjoy something more valuable later—is arguably the most important skill of all.

There's a famous social-science study called the Marshmallow Test, in which psychologist Walter Mischel isolated a series of children in their own private room with one

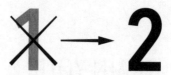

Resist one thing now, get two things later

marshmallow on a plate. Each child was told they had two options. They could eat that marshmallow immediately, or they
could wait and later the researchers would bring in another
marshmallow and they would get to eat both of them.

What is mind-blowing about this study is that Mischel
returned to his cohort many years later and looked at how
successful the kids who had the self-control not to eat the first
marshmallow had become, versus those kids who had not.

Astoundingly, he found that later in life, the children who
resisted eating marshmallow number one generally performed
better in school exams, had better social functioning, were
healthier and had higher self-esteem.

Mischel then spent decades studying the long-term
impact of having self-control and found that it led to higher
life satisfaction, greater self-respect, better career progress,
the ability to successfully quit smoking, and even how much
money people had in retirement.

Self-control is vital. And we as a species are becoming
weaker in this crucial area, owing to the ease of modern life.

Now the good news is that weak self-control is quite easy
to fix. If you focus on it.

Self-control is like a muscle; the more you use it, the
stronger it gets. So during the day look for small self-control

exercises that will gradually strengthen your ability to control impulses.

When you want to eat a snack, wait 30 minutes. If you want to leave work, stay for just a little longer. If you want two glasses of wine, settle for one. If you want to shout at someone, hold your tongue. If you don't want to exercise, force yourself to do at least a little.

Behaving this way is only mildly difficult, because each postponement of gratification is relatively minor and short-lived.

But cumulatively they will substantially increase your ability to master your immediate urges and develop mighty self-control, which, in my view, is one of the most under-appreciated and valuable skills of modern times.

WIN FAST ACTION STEPS

- Work out where your self-control issues are. They could be around food, being physically active, speaking unkindly to others, negative self-talk, laziness, sleeping too long or not enough, or any of a hundred areas of life.

- Decide on three easy ways you can strengthen your willpower and exert self-control.

- For the next month, focus on improving your control in those areas.

- The next month, pick a harder self-control issue to conquer, and so on, until you truly have become a master of willpower.

DO MEETINGS STANDING UP

Let's face it, long boring meetings
are the bane of most professional
people's existence.

But it's a double whammy: they're not just boring, they suck up the time you often needed to get other, more important work done.

Yes, most people concur that many meetings suck, but what amazes me is how few people try to do anything about it. It seems that society has collectively capitulated to the notion that meetings are always going to be a massive drain on our time and our workplace happiness.

But it doesn't have to be this way.

There are numerous ways to make meetings much shorter, while keeping—and in many cases enhancing—their effectiveness.

When I coach team managers, I am always exhorting them to focus on a series of powerful techniques for keeping meetings short and sharp.

One of the best ones is to do all but the most important meetings standing up.

I guarantee you, if you do meetings standing up you will at least halve the length of them. There will be no time-wasting chitchat before the meeting starts. People are far less likely to gasbag on and on about issues, and will get to the heart of the matter fast. And everyone will be much more focused on the agenda and the next discussion item.

What I love about this technique is that it is so simple and so easy to implement—you literally just walk into a meeting room and stay standing. There's no preparatory work needed, no software and no training necessary to make it instantly effective.

And doing it will save hundreds of hours a year for most people. Which in an entire organization means *tens of thousands of hours* saved.

Think about it this way. If you walked into the office of most bosses and said, "I know a way to save our company tens of thousands of hours of work. The method is free, easy and instant. Would that be of value to you?"

You know what the answer would be. "Hell yeah!"

Doing stand-up meetings is that way.

There's another benefit to the technique as well. Standing up for the duration of a meeting maintains every participant's energy levels. You know those terrible late-afternoon meetings where half the room is almost comatose with lethargy? That doesn't happen with a stand-up meeting. People are always much more awake, energetic and dynamic. Ideas come faster. Moods are more likely to be up. The whole vibe of the meeting is more vibrant.

Personally, I think maintaining an energized environment during meetings is crucial for both team morale and effective outcomes. It also makes work life loads more fun.

So the next time you have a meeting scheduled, ask the other attendees to give it a try. Make a stand and make them stand.

WIN FAST ACTION STEPS

- Give this meeting system three tries before you decide its worth to you.
- Consider having one meeting room with zero chairs.
- Start with relatively short and unimportant meetings first.

HAVE A BETWEEN LIST

This technique is really pro-level productivity stuff.

There are very few people who value their time so much that they embrace this type of technique, yet once you add it to your repertiore it's hard not to—the results are that immediate and compelling.

You will not only will get mountains of more tasks done, but also your stress levels will greatly reduce, as you clean up a lot of loose ends in your life and work.

The Between List is a very simple concept, but a profoundly impactful one. You keep a short list of things you could do for whenever a small window of extra time comes up in your day.

For example, all those occasions when a person you are meeting is running five minutes late, how do you spend that time?

Well, the average person does very little. Maybe they cruise their email, scroll through social media or hop online to see which celebrity has done something kooky.

But once you maintain an active Between List, you'll use those tiny blocks of time in very useful ways.

Here's how it works: Anytime that you think of a task that can be done in three minutes or less, you add it to your between list. At any one time there might be between five and ten items on it.

Then when a few spare minutes come up here and there, you use that time to work on those tasks and get them off your list.

Once you begin using this strategy, it will quickly become apparent how many unused, small blocks of time there actually are in a typical day.

Maybe you're waiting for a client to arrive. Or a conference to start. Or dinner to be on the table—or your spouse to finally be ready to go out!

Most people totally waste that time, but not you: you'll just get out your between list and knock off a few items.

I know it seems like a tiny amount of time to focus on, but I assure you: practice this system for a month and you'll be stunned by how much extra stuff you get done, with virtually no extra effort.

Achievement is a fascinating thing. Very often some of the most useful things you do are the quickest to actually complete. Many tasks literally take a few minutes, yet can make a massive difference to the quality of your life, your mood and your overall momentum—such as phoning a dear friend you haven't spoken to for ages, or booking a surprise dinner for your partner.

At the end of many days I am often amazed by the fact that some of the most valuable things I did that day were not time consuming. Achievement and time are often aligned but not always correlated.

The Between List unlocks many pods of time that were previously overlooked and brings them to life, filling your world with more success, enjoyment and connection.

And the next time you are stuck waiting for something or someone, it replaces feelings of irritation with that delicious feeling of making progress.

WIN FAST ACTION STEPS

- Buy a small notebook for your between list.
- Take it with you wherever you go, so that if you find you have a little spare time, you can quickly consult it and easily achieve some quick wins.

USE THE BEZOS
DECISION-MAKING SYSTEM

My work as a high-performance coach to high achievers usually consists of sharing with my clients two types of wisdom.

First, I share my own discoveries on how to maximize human performance that I've identified over three decades of pushing the boundaries in my own life.

And second, I teach my clients methods used by some of society's elite performers.

After all, I certainly don't have a monopoly on good ideas and I've found that as I continue to study high achievers in a myriad of fields, I keep discovering fabulous ways to achieve more, earn more and be more that I can pass onto my clients.

This particular technique falls into the latter category. It's used by Jeff Bezos, founder of Amazon and clearly one of the greatest business minds of all time. I think it's brilliant, and I urge you to use it whenever you need to make decisions in any area of your life.

Bezos categorizes decisions in two ways: Type One decisions and Type Two decisions.

Type One decisions are not easily reversible, so you must consider them extremely carefully and with great depth before you make them.

Type Two decisions are reversible: If you realize you've made a mistake you can get out of them relatively easily. Therefore they should be made relatively quickly.

The problem is, many people rush crucial Type One decisions, acting before they have fully considered every aspect of the situation. This can frequently lead to major disasters in both business and life.

And almost as bad, people can take ages deciding which way to go on Type Two decisions, when these are issues that could easily be reversed if they are found to be wrong, and so should be decided on promptly.

So the next time you have a key decision to make, ask yourself whether it falls into the Type One or Type Two category. And make your decision either quickly or with great care!

WIN FAST ACTION STEPS

- Look back on your last few recent decisions. Should any of them be reversed?
- Make a quick summary of any upcoming issues you need to decide upon.
- Categorize them as Type One or Type Two and act accordingly.

AIM TO BE IN THE TOP
10 PERCENT OF YOUR FIELD

*Have you ever noticed that the people at the
very top of any field get a disproportionately
large slice of the rewards?*

Think of top pop stars and what they earn compared to the moderately successful ones. Or the top plastic surgeons, executives or sports heroes. In any field, those regarded as the very best are not only the most sought after, they command vastly higher fees than everyone else.

It may not be fair, but it's a universal truth; the winners take all—or at least most—of the spoils.

With that in mind, don't you think it's extraordinary that so few people ever aim to be at the absolute top of their profession?

Most folks are quite happy to just do well in their jobs, seemingly unaware that if they aimed higher they could end up with ten times more in life.

More success. More money. More self-esteem. More freedom. More of just about everything that collectively as a species we view as desirable.

There's a reason that people aim low, of course. They

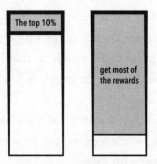

think it's too hard to get to the top and many believe they don't have what it takes to get there.

I beg to differ. I actually think getting into the top 10 percent of most fields is much easier than people think. I didn't say it was easy, just easier than people imagine.

Consider this: There are very few people actually aiming for the top, so the competition is much smaller than for those who aim to reach the middle.

Consider also that the people who are in the top 10 percent are never ten times better than average performers. In fact, they may only be 10 or 20 percent better. You may only have to lift your game a little to rise up the success ladder a lot further.

So how do you get into the top 10 percent of people in your industry?

First you have to aim for it.

Then you have to believe with all your heart that it's possible for you to achieve.

Next you have to study people who are currently in the top 10 percent. What do they do, how do they behave, how much effort do they put in, even what do they wear?

I am absolutely stunned by how many people profess that they want to reach the top of their profession yet have no idea whatsoever of what the people at that level actually do! Seriously, how can you hit a target when you don't even know what it is?

Then, having taken these three steps, you have to map out a plan on how you will bridge the gap between where you are now and where you want to be.

Then work that plan every day.

Look, you have to go to work anyway. Why not aim to be in at least the top 10 percent of your field?

By following these simple steps, you don't just hugely increase the chances of you getting into the top 10 percent, you also will enjoy your days at work a lot more, as well as win more of the financial rewards that are earned at this higher level. After all, going for greatness is a whole lot more exciting than going for slightly above average.

WIN FAST ACTION STEPS

- Identify three people who are at the top of your field.
- Identify the attributes these people share: skills, earnings, mindset.
- Decide which of these you need to work on.
- Focus on this list each week.

MAKE YOUR DESK LIKE THE SAHARA DESERT

The ideal mental state when you want to get things done is clear and relaxed.

But it's hard to have that state of mind when your desk is covered in papers, stationery and reports. The truth is, a messy work environment can lead to a messy, ineffective mind.

There are many tips for organizing your work life that I could give you, but the following three-minute exercise is the simplest, fastest and one of the most game-changing ways to lift your work performance to a higher level.

In the next three minutes I want you to do two things:

1. Throw out everything on your desk that isn't vital.
2. Get the rest off your desk. I don't care where you put it: in a drawer, a filing cabinet or a cupboard – just get it off your desk.

The only things on your desk should be your computer, your phone and the task you're working on right now. That's it.

Do this and your world will instantly become less stressed. You'll feel more in control because your environment is now under control. You will think more clearly. You will be less distracted. You will feel more motivated to work.

If you work in a company, an ultra minimal work environment will also make a major positive impression on the people around you—you'll look far more organized and on top of things than someone with papers and folders all over their desk.

Now, let's be frank. The reality is that we have only solved part of the organization productivity challenge. You still need to organize all that stuff you've stored away, but for now you have made a major leap forward.

Environment matters. It has a massive effect on your mind and your motivation. The human brain craves order and calm, and the more you clog up your environment with stimuli, the more anxious your mind will be.

Have you ever been to an ultra-luxurious health spa? Remember the amazing feeling of serenity and peace that you felt in there? It wasn't just because of the new-age music they were playing, it was also because in spas everything is neat, minimal, clean and clear. Just stepping into an environment like that soothes the soul and clears the head.

You need to make your desk the same. Super bare and minimal, so that each morning, when you walk into your work area, you are not overwhelmed by reminders of all the work you have to do and all the responsibilities that rest on your shoulders.

The world is complex enough. Create clarity and peace on your desk and you'll experience a similar clarity and peace in your mind.

WIN FAST ACTION STEPS

- Create your Sahara desk in two stages.
- Make a substantial improvement immediately by clearing everything not required right now from your desk—just put it on the floor or in a cupboard. Enjoy an increased sense of serenity.
- Then set a time in your calendar to spend 20 minutes clearing and storing those items properly.
- Consider buying an in-tray so that new items are temporarily quarantined in one neat place.

INCREASE YOUR BRAINPOWER WITH BAROQUE MUSIC

We have all experienced our brain being affected by music.

Whether it's scary music in a horror movie, motivating music in a gym or romantic music in a restaurant, it's clear that the human brain is quickly changed by the music it hears.

But there is one type of music that has more of an effect on you than any other music tested: Baroque music.

What is Baroque music exactly? Well, it's classical music from the Baroque period, which was between around 1600 to 1750.

And what makes it so effective for your mind's functioning? Well, most Baroque music pulses between 50 to 80 beats per minute, and this has a major effect on your brainwaves.

There have been countless studies done on how the human brain is influenced by music of this period, but here are just a few of the results:

- People pick up languages faster when Baroque music is played. (Check out the work of Georgi Lozanov and

his incredible accelerated learning
language system.)
- Slow Baroque music such as Handel
  or Vivaldi has been shown to increase
  creativity. (In university tests both in
  Australia and the Netherlands.)
- Students working with Baroque music in
  the background found math challenges
  easier.
- Baroque tunes have been shown to
  enhance brainpower in babies.

Pretty much any area of your thinking seems to be positively affected by this extraordinarily influential music, so it's a no-brainer that you start using it in your own life to achieve better results.

Here's my technique.

As soon as you begin your day, play some Baroque music for ten to fifteen minutes. You'll find that after a short while your mood lifts and your mind sharpens. I like to play it as soon as I enter my office, while I'm sorting out my To-Do lists and getting ready for the day's work.

Another time I find it works really well is mid-afternoon, when I'm sometimes feeling a bit lethargic. I often use one of the music concentration apps such as Focus @ Will for a similar afternoon mental pick-me-up.

In this hypercompetitive world we need to use every good method we can to maximize our personal performance.

Baroque music is one of the easiest and most enjoyable ways to do exactly that.

WIN FAST ACTION STEPS

- Search online for some "best of Baroque" music collections, then buy or download one.
- Once you get used to having Baroque music in the background, expand your collection.
- Think of three situations when having Baroque music playing in the background would work well for you.

THINK GAME, NOT WAR

There are two ways you can achieve great success.
The stressful way and the enjoyable way.

Strangely, most people choose the stressful way.

This is a matter of cultural conditioning. They have been conditioned by society to think that high achievement can only be pulled off with enormous amounts of stress and effort. There is currently a whole culture in the business world around "hustling," a term that has come to mean working insane hours and pushing yourself to your limits in the belief that this is the only path to making it in life.

When you think about it deeply, it's an absurd notion—as illogical as saying that an artist could create a much better painting by applying more paint to their picture. Hard work (or paint) is necessary, but it's what you do with it that really matters.

But more insidious than the current obsession with long work hours is the emotional state that accompanies it. Many people seem to feel that the whole work thing should be emotionally taxing. They see winning at work and life as a war. A war between them and their competitors. A war between their desires and their self-discipline. A war between who they are now and who they dream of becoming.

In my view, this is not just an incorrect paradigm, but an exceedingly dangerous one. It encourages one of the primary killers of humans in the world today: prolonged stress.

If you subconsciously believe that life is a war that you must win, then your mind and body will respond to that—by exuding stress.

Ironically you can achieve as much in life—if not more—by making one small but pivotal change in your mental makeup.

Seeing life not as war, but as a game.

A game can still be played at a very high level, but people who see what they do as a game bring a certain level of joy, excitement and fun to the whole endeavor. Simultaneously, they are applying ultra-high standards to what they are doing.

In business, Richard Branson is a great example of this. Few people on the planet have achieved as much in business, but Branson has always emphasized that he sees his work as the ultimate fun game.

In science, great physicists like Albert Einstein and Richard Feynman were similar—eager to excel at the topmost levels but having a whole lot of fun in the process.

Billionaire investor Warren Buffett says he enjoys his work so much that he "tap dances to work" every morning.

So what about you? Do you see what you do more as a war or a game?

In my view, one way of thinking leads to a stressful life

whereas the other leads to a life of adventure and invigorating challenge.

It's important to emphasize that both ways can be played at a high level. But each one leads to an entirely different feeling.

If upon consideration you feel that you may have been focusing too much on the "life is a war" paradigm, then consider spending the next two weeks bringing an attitude of lightness and play to your work.

If you ask me, it's a much better way to live.

WIN FAST ACTION STEPS

- In your world, what would someone who treated life like a game be like?
- How specifically would they behave?
- What areas of your life do you most need to add that lighter, fun spirit to?

BREAK YOUR BAD HABITS
WITH THE WIPE SYSTEM

We all have some bad habits. Some, like indulging in too many slices of chocolate cake at birthday parties, are nothing to worry about. Others, though, may be putting a ceiling on your success and happiness.

I'm going to give you a two-step system that, if you stick to it, will get rid of most bad habits.

It's called the wipe system.

With this method you need to come up with an alternative solution to the current bad habit and embed it into your mind.

Most habits are classic stimulation/response scenarios. When you're in a certain place or situation, you automatically do the habit.

Over time you have developed physical neural pathways in your brain that ensure that when a particular situation happens you strongly desire to do the habit. I'm being literal here. That thought pattern is now actually *physically* wired into your brain.

Smokers are a classic example of this. So many people I know are fine with not smoking—until they have a drink at

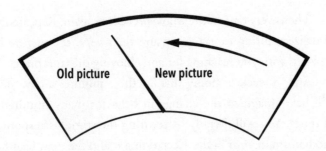

a party! That situation immediately makes them respond by seeking out a cigarette.

So step one of the wipe system is thinking of some alternative activity instead of the bad habit.

For example, if you are addicted to eating ice cream late at night, you should buy packets of frozen fruit pieces and put them in your freezer—they are similar to ice cream, in that they are very cold and very sweet.

Step two is mentally rehearsing making the switch from reaching for the dreaded ice cream to the fruit pieces whenever you go to the freezer.

To achieve this you close your eyes and imagine that you want to eat ice cream and you are walking to your fridge. Then I want you to imagine that a car's windshield wiper goes across that picture in your mind and wipes it away and immediately replaces it with a picture of you reaching for fruit pieces and really enjoying them.

As the mental windshield wiper replaces the ice cream picture with the fruit picture, I want you to say to yourself, "Wipe."

This exercise only a takes a few seconds, so I want you to spend three minutes repeatedly carrying it out.

Then every day do the whole procedure again. Repeatedly visualize wanting to eat ice cream, then *wipe*, the picture is replaced with you reaching for and enjoying the fruit pieces.

After a week of doing this for three minutes a day, you will have imagined the change in behavior many hundreds of times. You will literally be rewiring the stimulus/response mechanism in your brain. Keep doing it and the new, healthier behavior will become automatic.

Radical, I know. But for most bad habits, really effective.

WIN FAST ACTION STEPS

- Try the wipe system right now, in the next two minutes. Just pick any issue you'd like to work on and get started.

- The aim of acting immediately on this is not to totally solve that particular issue but just to get you used to using this amazing method.

IF YOU WANT TO STOP FEELING MISERABLE, STOP THINKING OF YOURSELF

If you are constantly feeling down about your life, there is a highly effective tactic that hardly anybody uses.

Stop spending so much time thinking about yourself.

In many cases (but certainly not all), one of the main reasons some people are consistently miserable is that they endlessly ruminate about their own lives.

They obsessively think about what's going wrong in their life—and who's to blame.

The antidote is a simple one: Start spending most of your day trying to help other people. By focusing on helping others, several very important changes take place in your mind.

- The amount of time you are thinking about your own troubles greatly diminishes. The less time you think about your own problems, generally the more hours of the day you will be happier.

- If you help people less fortunate than yourself, you inevitably begin to feel better about your own life. As the psychologist and well-being researcher Tim Kasser showed, comparison with others is a crucial determinant of your own happiness, and this is perfectly expressed in a Persian proverb: "I wept because I had no shoes, until I saw the man who had no feet."
- The very act of being altruistic makes people happier. At the University of Pennsylvania, researchers have tested this. People who perform just one altruistic act are usually demonstrably happier for the rest of the day.

Think about that last one for a moment. A single act of kindness can make you feel good for the whole day? Imagine the impact of your own mental state if you filled much of your year with kind acts.

I'm not talking about giving up your usual life and wandering the streets performing saintly acts. But rather, imagine being around your family or going to work as usual, but changing your primary motivation to simply being of service to everyone around you. That is enough to take your focus off yourself and to place it onto others.

By the way, if you do this in your workplace, you won't just be happier, you'll be more successful, too.

I know that all kinds of psychologists will say there are numerous other factors that lead to people feeling habitually miserable, and I don't deny this.

But in my view, altruism and forgetting about your own problems is greatly underrated as a pathway to feeling fabulous.

WIN FAST ACTION STEPS

- Think of some people who you could help. They may be friends, associates or any underprivileged people that you know of. Reach out to them.

- Call up a nearby charity and offer your services for a few hours a week.

- Consider giving blood and search online for the closest donor center to you.

DO AN INDECISION PURGE

*One of the biggest roadblocks to high achievement
is the dark, insidious force of indecision.*

I have seen men and woman virtually paralyzed by indecision, totally unable to move forward in any direction, so beset are they by confusion about which path they should follow.

There is no peace of mind when you are undecided. The feeling of uncertainty gnaws away at you, progressively sapping your confidence and obliterating your momentum.

Sometimes for years.

You must confront indecision in your life and destroy it every chance you can.

Now, I'm not talking about rushing decisions, not at all. (See the advice on how to decide intelligently, using the Bezos decision-making system on page 82).

I'm talking about when you have been avoiding making a decision for an extended period of time, when the facts are known. This kind of procrastination needs to be rooted out of your life, for the simple reason that it drags on your ability to progress.

For many people reading this book, the single most

potent move you can make to improve your momentum is to identify any issues that you are of two minds about and make a decision.

In order to do so, there are three ways of thinking that will help you.

The first is to remember that if you have been ruminating on an issue for ages but not acted on it, in all likelihood you do not need more information, despite what you may think. You're far better off deciding now with the information you already have, and moving on.

The second thing to keep in mind is the reason you have been unable to decide is probably because either option is pretty good. (This has helped me a lot.)

Third, if it's a business decision, appreciate that if you wait for all the data that's possible to get before committing to a direction, your competitors will leave you in the dust. In today's business world, speed is of prime importance. As one of the greatest generals of modern warfare, George Patton, said: "A good plan violently executed now is better than a perfect plan next week."

Your first move in initiating an Indecision Purge is to evaluate each of the major areas of your life, searching for where indecision is limiting your ability to move forward.

With your health, are there any areas in which you are undecided? Consider diet, gym memberships, sleep, going ahead with a surgical operation etc.

How about business? What areas are you considering and reconsidering endlessly? It could be hiring, leaving a company, promoting someone, considering further training—issues of that nature.

Are there any unresolved issues in your spiritual life? Maybe you're considering reconnecting with your church, or adopting a new faith altogether. Or perhaps you want to study the great spiritual texts, but can't decide which ones.

What about your love life? There's usually a handful of decisions lying dormant there.

Then, of course, there are the social, recreational and fun aspects of life; places you've always wanted to vacation but just haven't committed to yet; friendships you want to cultivate or uncouple from.

Once you decide one way or the other in every gray area of your life, you will experience a great weight off your mind. Life will become clearer, simpler and happier.

When you decide to decide, you free yourself to achieve more, earn more and be more.

WIN FAST ACTION STEPS

- Allocate ten minutes to do a quick audit of your life. Look for any part where procrastination is inhibiting progress.

- Set a one-hour time slot in your calendar entitled "Decision Time!" and make all the decisions at once. It will be scary but liberating.

PUT ON SOMEONE ELSE'S HEAD

One of the most crucial skills in today's world is fresh thinking.

The more originally you think, the better chance you have of conceiving ideas that are brilliant and way above what your competition is thinking.

But thinking unusually is hard work. It's tough to think with true originality.

I have spent decades of my life as a professional thinker. As a creative director in advertising agencies, I only got paid when I produced excellent ideas, so over the years I learned some potent ways to come up with great concepts and solutions.

I'd like to teach you one of my most effective ways right now.

But first a warning. What I'm about to teach you is pretty weird stuff. You may think I'm a little crazy for suggesting this method. But trust me, it really works if you want to think brilliantly and differently.

Okay, here's the technique.

The next time you are stuck for ideas, you need to pretend

you are someone else. But not just anyone, one of the greatest humans of all time.

For example, ask yourself, "How would Richard Branson solve this?" Then sit at your desk and imagine you are taking off your head. Then imagine you are replacing your head with Richard Branson's head.

Literally pretend you are him solving your problem.

Now take off Branson's head and put on Bill Gates's head. How would he solve your problem? Spend at least five minutes as Bill Gates.

Every five or ten minutes, change your head to other famous people. Picasso. Or General Colin Powell.

How would Mark Cuban come up with a solution? Put on his head and try to think like him. What would Madonna do in your situation? Put on her head and actually be her for a while.

At first it seems ridiculous to pretend you are someone else, especially someone famous. But stick with it and really commit to the process and you will experience an amazing transformation.

You'll start to come up with ideas that will totally surprise you. And many of them will be outstanding.

Why does this technique work? Well, if you fully commit, it frees your mind from your habitual ways of thinking to explore completely new approaches to solve problems. It awakens usually dormant powers. It enables you to perceive the problem from completely different directions.

It unlocks your higher genius.

It's also beneficial if you have a low self-image when it comes to your intelligence or creativity. You may not view yourself as particularly creative, but I'm sure you believe others are.

So become someone else for a while and watch "their" brilliant solutions come through to you.

WIN FAST ACTION STEPS

- Come up with a list of five people whose head you'd like to use.
- Pick a current challenge that would benefit from some fresh thinking.
- Spend six minutes as each one and see what results "they" create.
- Stay open and committed during the process.

KNOW YOUR TWO CIRCLES OF CONTROL

When you're under stress with a mountain of work to do, it's easy to get flustered and depressed.

But there's a potent technique you can use that virtually immediately reduces your stress and gets you focused on really solving your work challenges.

I call it the two circles of control.

Here's the gist of it:

Whenever you're stressed by a situation, draw two large circles on a piece of paper. These we will call the Can't Control and Can Control circles.

Inside the circle on the left write in all the things you cannot control about the situation.

For example, if you are having problems with your boss because they are always giving you unfair deadlines while also badmouthing you to the CEO, in the Can't Control circle you write "my boss's poor character," "my boss's inefficiency," "working with crazy deadlines" etc.

Then in the circle on the right, write in all the elements of the situation that you can control.

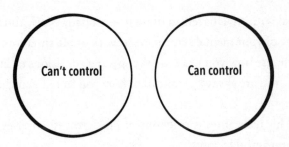

Examples of these might include "my positive attitude," "my calmness," "improving my direct relationship with the CEO," "whether I stay or leave this company," "my organizational abilities," "my sense of humor" etc.

Then look at these two circles several times during the day and resolve to only focus your thoughts and actions on things in the Can Control circle.

It's such a good technique because it reminds you to spend all your time on the things you can actually do to improve the situation—and stop spending time worrying about things you can't control or even affect much anyway.

It really relieves your stress levels, too.

It's also an outstanding technique because highly successful people do not let their negative emotions get in the way of doing an excellent job, whatever they're working on. Looking at your two circles of control often helps you to remember that just because a situation is bad doesn't mean you have to feel bad while you're in it. There are always positive steps you can take.

You are not a puppet of circumstances. You can choose to maintain your happiness and sense of humor, even if you have to deal with Machiavellian dimwits on a daily basis. You're in charge of your mental state in every work or life situation. You can choose how you react to other people's decisions or ineptitude. You are always in control of how you feel, if you choose to be.

This realization is truly one of life's great discoveries and most powerful lessons.

So next time you're feeling down about something, or you get a setback at work, take a few minutes to create your two circles of control.

Then spend every minute you can focusing on things inside the Can Control circle. It will radically improve both your effectiveness and your happiness.

WIN FAST ACTION STEPS

- After creating your first two circles of control, stick them up somewhere where you'll see them often – on your bathroom mirror, in your wardrobe, in the kitchen or on your computer. If you don't want other people to see your circles, put them on small cards and keep them in your pocket.

- As part of your evening review, consider asking yourself about how long you spent in your Can Control circle that day.

DO A ONE-MINUTE
BRAIN REBOOT

*Computers work better after a reboot,
why not do the same with your brain?*

If you've been having an unusually stressful day and still have a few hours of work to go, it's vital that you get yourself to reduce the tension, clear your head and start thinking optimally again.

The good news is this can be achieved in just 60 seconds, simply by using the Brain Reboot method.

Here's how to reset your brain so you can win fast for the rest of the day.

Find yourself a quiet place where you will be undisturbed for a minute or so. It could be your office, or if you're a stressed-out parent, maybe escape to the bathroom at home and shut the door.

Now close your eyes and imagine a computer plug disconnected from the power point on a wall. Next imagine the picture in your mind going totally black.

Hold that picture of a black screen in your mind for around a minute and breathe deeply and slowly, letting go of your stress with every out breath.

Then imagine your hand reconnecting the computer plug to the power point in the wall and see and feel your brain coming back to life, refreshed and ready to go.

Wham! You've just done a Brain Reboot.

You may have to do this a few times to feel comfortable with it, but once you get used to it, you'll learn to love these brain reboots.

Even though the whole process only takes about 60 seconds, you will be pleasantly surprised by what a difference it makes to the state of your mood and mind.

The truth is, your brain doesn't need an hour to stop and recover from stressful or negative situations, it's way more powerful than that. Everyone's brain is eminently capable of completely relaxing and reinvigorating in a minute or less— but it needs two things: your belief that change can happen this quickly and a good method for making it happen.

You now have that method.

When are good times to use the Brain Reboot?

Just after a tough phone call. Just before a big meeting or presentation. Just after you've had to deal with a frustrating situation. Just before you go to bed at night.

Pretty much whenever you feel less than your normal self.

In the future, I believe millions of ambitious people will use techniques like the brain reboot to optimize their performance and increase their chances of winning faster. But if you can utilize these techniques now, years before most people even know about them, you'll have a fabulous advantage over your competitors.

Your brain is your ultimate tool for achieving your dreams. Don't just use it in an average, low-level way. I urge you to constantly look for ways to unlock your brain's truly awesome powers to get you what you want in life. The Brain Reboot method is a fabulous way to start doing that.

WIN FAST ACTION STEPS

- Try the Brain Reboot once now, even if you don't feel the need to reboot your mind.
- Use slow, deep breathing as you do it.
- Think of three situations that occur regularly where you could use the Reboot.

GET RID OF 50 PERCENT OF YOUR POSSESSIONS

Owning lots of stuff may not seem like it lowers your chances of success, but I believe it does for several key reasons.

For a start, owning lots of stuff stops you finding what you need quickly.

When you really need to find something and you can't, it can be stressful and frustrating.

How many times have you searched desperately for something as you are running out of time to get somewhere important? That's a terrible feeling, but many people experience it almost every week.

When you don't own much, you find things quickly and easily.

Second, you think more clearly when you live in a minimalist environment.

When your desk, company premises, bedroom and living areas at home are devoid of clutter, it definitely calms the mind. Life is busy enough without making your environment busy as well.

Look at virtually every top performer in life and you will see that their immediate environment is not messy and cluttered. (There are exceptions, of course, as there are for any rule, but it's true in a high percentage of cases.)

Finally, owning few possessions makes you appreciate each one that you have.

When you own mountains of stuff, it's tricky to feel genuinely passionate about each and every item. When you get rid of extraneous belongings—anything that is not of quality, that you don't really need or have a fondness for, or see in your future—then what remains is much more valuable to you. You notice it, appreciate it and utilize it much more.

A lot of this is about maintaining a philosophy of excellence about your environment. I believe that a person's life can be completely transformed by adopting an overall philosophy of excellence in every aspect of their life. By simply making the decision to do everything as excellently as you can (in the time allotted), your life takes on a much higher success trajectory.

Your home and work environments are two of the best places to start when adopting this life philosophy. Reducing your possessions by 50 percent in these two areas will have a gigantic effect on your clarity of thought, your serenity and your quality of life.

Your possessions affect you mentally, emotionally and even physically. Dramatically reducing the number of them is definitely one of the most powerful ways to upgrade your mind and your results.

WIN FAST ACTION STEPS

- Start by setting a timer for 30 minutes, then getting rid of as much stuff as you can around your office.
- Then allocate four more 30-minute periods and remove as much as you can from your wardrobe, garage or storage area, bathroom and then kitchen.
- After you have undertaken these initial purges, come back to each area over the next two weeks until you have eliminated around 50 percent of what was there originally in each.

GET THE TRUTH FROM YOUR FRIENDS

I'm a big fan of optimism, but there's one place we should avoid it as much as possible.

When we are evaluating our own performance.

According to research conducted by social psychologist David Dunning while at Cornell University, most of us are outrageously optimistic when it comes to judging our own abilities.

As Dunning has shown over many years of research, we tend to think we are smarter than we are, and more creative than we are, and that we will be more successful than we end up being.

We can be highly self-delusional about our talents and aptitudes.

If we want to win more in life, clearly we need to get a more accurate picture of what our abilities truly are, as well as what flaws we have, in order to eradicate them and take our performance to a higher level.

How do we do that? We need to ask the people around us what we are *really* like. We need feedback from objective sources to counter our own bias for believing we are better than we actually are.

Easier said than done, of course, as so many of our friends and colleagues would rather say nice things about us than tell us the truth.

That's why it's important to ask them in a certain way that makes them feel comfortable about telling us how it really is.

Here's a good way to do it.

Pick between five and ten of your friends or work associates that you have a good relationship with. You don't have to be best buddies with them, but you should get on well with each of them and you should feel that they are genuine supporters of and believers in you.

Then write them an email saying several things: that you are always trying to improve yourself, that you really value their opinion (they'll like that), and that you'd really appreciate it if they could give you an honest answer to three simple questions.

1. What are my strengths?
2. What are my weaknesses?
3. How could I be a better version of me?

That's all you need to ask them. Keep it simple and easy for them to respond to and you're much more likely to receive honest feedback.

When you get the answers back, don't necessarily take them as gospel. Each are, after all, only one person's opinion. But look mostly for repetition. If two or more people write the same thing about you, then there's a good chance it's something you should take note of.

This feedback is not bulletproof as a methodology, but it will really open your eyes to how you truly are performing at work and in life.

It's can be a scary and confronting exercise, but it's so worthwhile. The most elite performers in the world, in any field, only got there because they ruthlessly addressed any aspect of their performance that wasn't first rate and then deliberately and consistently worked at refining themselves in those areas.

You need to do the same.

WIN FAST ACTION STEPS

- Choose five friends you can immediately reach out to.
  - Spend a few minutes preparing what you will say to them.
- Email them and ask them to come back to you within forty-eight hours with their answers.
  - Once you have your feedback and identified the common points people say about you, spend ten minutes thinking about how you can rectify your weaknesses.

MAKE YOUR USUAL ANSWER "YES"

Some years ago I realized that anyone could hugely improve the quality of their life by making one simple change to what they did.

What is the change that has such a significant impact on our enjoyment of life?

When in doubt, say "Yes."

When you're not sure whether to accept that dinner invitation, say "Yes."

When you are of two minds about saying hello to that acquaintance, say "Yes" and walk up to them.

When you're not certain you have the ability to go for that job, say "Yes" and apply.

If you are not sure you have time to start that hobby, say "Yes" and give it a go.

If friends invite you to a party, say "Yes" every time.

Saying "Yes" as a matter of habit, as a clear personal philosophy, completely alters your life.

You experience more amazing moments, meet more special people, increase your chances of a magnificent romance, get more business opportunities, massively increase your

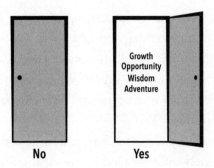

number of influential contacts, hear about many more brilliant business ideas, hear a lot more funny jokes and create thousands more wonderful memories.

However, if you habitually say "No" when you're unsure about doing something, you may be right on occasion, but you also miss out on so many positive experiences, opportunities and fun.

Now, of course, it's not easy to make this your embedded way of operating. There is more risk, more uncertainty and in many cases, more stress. But it leads to a much bigger and more exciting life.

People who say "No" as a matter of habit have a lot more safety and a lot more certainty in their lives. And their lives are often much calmer. But they also spend a lot more time home watching TV, going to the same old places with the same old friends.

There is a great movie about this very issue: *Yes Man*, starring Jim Carrey in which he plays a guy who is stuck in his negative ways, then goes to a self-help seminar and is transformed by the concept of saying "Yes" to everything.

Which brings up an important point. Am I suggesting you blindly do everything and take every opportunity that comes your way? Not at all. If you are clear that you don't want to do something, don't do it. What I'm saying is if you are undecided about whether to say "Yes" or "No," then make your default answer "Yes."

This one small change in how you make decisions opens up a completely different (and in my view, infinitely better) life.

I like the 90-Year Test. When deciding what to do about anything, just ask yourself, "When I'm 90 years old and I look back on my life, what kind of life will I wish I had led?"

A life of safety and certainty? Or a life of adventures, big and small?

Saying "Yes" instantly creates that life of adventure.

WIN FAST ACTION STEPS

- Think of three areas of your life or work where you need to make decisions.
- If you're genuinely undecided, just say "Yes" and get ready for the adventure.

GET SERIOUS ABOUT CELEBRATION

If you're ambitious to succeed at an unusually high level, you will experience disappointment regularly, as you inevitably fail to meet your own aims and standards.

The first thing you should remember about this is that it's absolutely normal. Failure is not only usual, it's absolutely necessary for you to discern how you should improve.

I actually wrote an entire book about this subject, *Why People Fail.*

You need to see failure as a must, and nothing to be at all ashamed of or worried about. If you are not regularly failing to meet your goals, then you should probably upgrade those goals.

As the great race car driver Mario Andretti said, "If everything seems under control, you're just not going fast enough."

But there can be a dark side to constantly going hard for big goals, and it is this:

We can become so focused on creating future results that we often forget to smell the roses and enjoy present-day life. We end up always striving and never arriving.

When I opened my first company in my early twenties, one of my business partners had a big sticker near his desk. It simply said, "Don't postpone joy." At the time I didn't think much about it, but as the years have gone by and I've matured, the sentiment of that sticker has impacted me increasingly.

If we attach all our happiness to the possible occurrence of a future event, then we are hardwiring ourselves for misery. Or at the very least a life of dissatisfaction.

That's why we must take celebration seriously.

Most success-oriented people don't celebrate nearly enough. Almost as soon as we achieve a goal, we start work on the next one. That's a huge mistake. If we took more time to celebrate our wins—even small ones—then the quality of our lives would improve markedly.

We'd enjoy our work a lot more, because it wouldn't be merely an endless series of challenges with no relief. We could give ourselves permission to stop for a few hours and pat ourselves on the back for a job well done.

It's not just good for us, if we celebrate at work; it's fabulous for the morale of our team, too. As one of the most famous CEOs of all time, Jack Welch, put it: "Celebrating makes people feel like winners and creates an atmosphere of recognition and positive energy."

So next time you reach a key goal, crack open a bottle of champagne and toast your achievement. Or go to a nice restaurant with your workmates. Or book a weekend away with your partner or family as a reward for all the hard work you've undertaken.

Life is short and true victories are few. Don't let another one go by without a major celebration.

WIN FAST ACTION STEPS

- Think of something that you or those around you have recently achieved.
- Think of a fun way to celebrate it with friends or associates.
- Prepare a short, inspiring speech about the celebration and then enjoy every moment of it.

DO ONE-MINUTE WORKOUTS

The prevailing opinion of experts on how much exercise you need to be physically fit is three periods of at least 30 minutes a week.

I think that's hogwash. You can stay fit in much less time.

Sure, in a perfect world you should do that level of exercise, and even more, but we don't live in such a world. If you find that it has been weeks since you've exercised, then I'd like to offer you a much more palatable and realistic alternative.

Exercise for one minute, whenever you have a little bit of time to spare.

Don't scoff. You can do a lot of good for your body in just one minute.

Go full-on and do it right and in a single 60-second session you can do any of the following:

- 40 push ups
- 30 sit ups
- 4 short, intense sprints
- 12 pull-ups

- 50 jumping jacks
- 25 leg squats

In one minute you can stretch all your major muscle groups. You could do 25 deep breaths and fully oxygenate your body.

Imagine you created a system of doing just five One-Minute Workouts during the day. One for stretching in the morning, one for push-ups, one for sit-ups, one for leg squats and one for sprints.

The "experts" can say what they like, but I've actually done this each day to test it, and found that my body responds amazingly. Aerobic capacity rises significantly. Arms, legs and stomach muscles get stronger. You become way more limber and your lung capacity improves markedly.

In just five minutes of exercise!

Yes, three lots of 30 minutes of standard exercise may get you a better result, and of course I recommend it over doing nothing. But most people simply do not have the time, discipline or the inclination to follow this regime, or anywhere close to it.

By the way, there's a growing body of evidence that indicates that short bursts of intense exercise have a much greater improvement on your health than long periods of moderate exercise. Google "HIIT training effects" and see for yourself.

This book is about how to win fast. To get extraordinary results quickly in your life, you are going to have to do some radical things. Business as usual just won't cut it. So give the

One-Minute Workouts a try and watch how quickly your body gets fitter, stronger and healthier.

WIN FAST ACTION STEPS

- Think of the three one-minute exercises you'd most like to do.
- Aim to do all three once a day for the next three days.
- Look for moments in between tasks where you can slip in a One-Minute Workout.
- Keep a set of hand weights near your desk.

ALWAYS LOOK FOR THE LIMITING FACTOR

In the early 1980s a management
consultant by the name of Eli Goldratt created a
way of improving how to manufacture
goods. He called it the Theory of Constraints.

While it was primarily meant to solve manufacturing and engineering challenges, in my opinion you can apply the Theory of Constraints to doing virtually anything better.

It's a really neat framework that you can use to fix almost any roadblock you are experiencing, in your company or in your personal life.

My version of the theory is as follows.

In any business or personal situation where you're encountering challenges, there will always be one main factor blocking your progress. This is known as the constraint.

So the first step is to identify the key constraint in whatever scenario that's proving difficult for you.

Once you've identified the main constraint, you need to focus with great intensity on this one area, applying all the resources and effort you can to eliminate or fix it quickly. Don't spend significant amounts of time concerning yourself with any other problems for now, just laser in on fixing this single limiter. Time spent on any other activities is never as fruitful as spending it on the one key constraint.

When you've fixed the key constraint by throwing everything you can at it, you move on to the next most important limiter to your progress, and so on, until all constraints have been dealt with.

At that point you look at another part of your life or work and look for the key constraint there.

No matter what the system or circumstances, there will always be something else that limits your progress in it.

It's a disarmingly simple model, but it can change your life if you consistently apply it.

You'll become a constraint-seeking and -destroying machine. You'll be able to walk into any situation and immediately know what to do to fix it: locate the constraint, devote total focus to eliminating that constraint, then look for the next constraint to home in on.

The Theory of Constraints simplifies your thinking enormously, particularly in complex situations. It creates great clarity of thought and massively increases the speed at which you can create improvement.

It's an awesome weapon against sloppy and unfocused problem solving.

WIN FAST ACTION STEPS

- Think about the biggest challenge you are currently having in your professional or personal life.
- What is the primary constraint you are facing?
- Come up with as many ways as possible to address this one area, until you fix it.
- Now look again at your situation. What is the next limiter to things being absolutely perfect?
- Repeat the process.

COMPARE YOURSELF TO THE BEST, NOT THE NEAREST

*Most people say talent is a wonderful
thing to possess.
I have seen it ruin many people.*

I have watched countless men and women become lazy and unmotivated to achieve great things because they were so damn talented that they could get away with not trying. If they were not so blessed with natural gifts, they would have been forced to try with all their heart, and as a result would have achieved much more in life.

Then there's the dangerous middle. People who are doing just fine, maybe even pretty well, compared to others around them. Because they look around and see that they are performing better than their immediate geographic competition, it lulls them into a sense of security and superiority and they begin to slow down and put their lives on cruise control.

This scenario is particularly acute for those who live in smaller cities or towns. They become the proverbial big fish in a small pond, and their benchmark for judging what is outstanding can actually be quite low.

Your competition

That's why it's imperative that if you want to win at a high level you must do two very important things.

1. Research who are the very best in your entire field, not just in your community or city, but in the whole world.
2. Focus on working at this global elite standard, not the standard of those close by.

I mentor people from many different industries and, in 90 percent of cases, I find that they have almost no idea who are the best performers in their industry even in their own city, let alone their state, their nation or other countries.

But if you want to live up to your full potential, you must know what that potential is. You must be totally cognizant of the world's best in your field. You must then study what they do, how they think, what they charge and how they differ from the rest.

It's never been easier to do this. When I started out in my career, there was no internet. I had to find out who the best were in my field of advertising by searching for books and magazines to locate the wizards of the industry in London, New York, Brazil and Singapore. That wasn't so easy when living in faraway Australia. But now in minutes you can locate the royalty of every industry with just an hour or two spent searching online.

Once you do locate your industry's legends, they must be the standard that you hold yourself to.

When you evaluate your work at the highest level, everything will change.

Your results. Your earnings. Your self-esteem.

WIN FAST ACTION STEPS

- Search online and ask your peers until you locate three of the top performers in your industry in the country.
  - Then identify three of the elite in your field worldwide. Do this by looking online at the other main English-speaking countries.
- Study three things: how they think, how they work and how they market themselves or their company.

BE YOUR OWN
MOTIVATION COACH

Imagine that you could have a top motivation coach
working with you 24/7.

Every time you felt down, your coach would inspire you with positive and encouraging words, lifting you up and keeping you performing at an ultra-high level.

Well, you can have such a motivation coach.

It's you.

As a high-performance coach, I have studied the field of human excellence deeply, for decades. And I've deduced that there's one area of motivation that is best done by the person themselves, not by any outside coach or mentor. This type of mental conditioning must be done by you to you, and when done well it can be pivotal in improving your performance in absolutely any field of endeavour.

The technique is known in sports psychology circles as your self-talk.

It's incredibly important and for the most part surprisingly simple to apply (although at times it can present challenges).

Self-talk is using your internal monologue to speak to yourself in a supportive, positive and uplifting manner.

Including, and especially, when events are not going to your liking.

After all, anybody can be positive when things are going fabulously. It takes no special skill to do that. But disciplining yourself to consistently speak to yourself in an encouraging way—a way that's much more likely to lead to you performing well soon after—well, that's a whole different ball game.

The majority of people are very bad at self-talk. Very often we talk ourselves down, not up. When things don't go well, we can beat ourselves up, blaming and complaining to ourselves about our own perceived inadequacies. If not halted, this negative self-berating leads to low self-esteem, a weak self-image and a correspondingly mediocre level of achievement.

Your self-talk really matters. You must make it a priority to talk positively to yourself and be your own best motivation coach.

I can assure you that almost all elite sportspeople are excellent at talking to themselves positively. They have been trained to do so. I also know that in elite military units (like the US Navy SEALs or the army's Delta Force) they teach and insist on positive self-talk.

How do you do self-talk well?

Every morning, evening and at regular intervals throughout the day, use your internal monologue to say short, positive sentences that rally your spirits and encourage you to believe in yourself and help you choose to behave in a manner befitting a high achiever.

Examples of self-talk include: "Keep going, you can do this," "This is easy," "I am smart and quick," "I get things done fast," "I earn XXXX dollars a year," "I am feeling terrific today" and "Smooth and easy."

One of the most useful exercises you can do is to take ten minutes to write down some self-talk expressions that you predict will help you stay on track. Then condition yourself to repeat them throughout each day.

Remember, you will perform largely in accordance with your thoughts. And your thoughts are closely correlated with your self-talk. So it pays to get this right.

WIN FAST ACTION STEPS

- Write down seven positive self-talk sentences that will help you feel and perform better.
- Start each morning saying each one three times, with commitment and belief.
- As you say them, feel inside that you truly embody the spirit of each phrase.
- Two or three times per day, or whenever you feel down, spend a minute or so repeating your statements.

RUSH THE UNIMPORTANT

In the field of productivity, this is one tactic that is rarely discussed.

Yet it is possibly the most effective technique of all for achieving at a stellar level.

Everyone in time-management circles talks about doing the important tasks first, which is indisputably good advice.

But that leaves all the other tasks. How are we supposed to complete them? Many people make a huge mistake in this regard, by doing these unimportant tasks well and carefully.

Now that sounds like a good way to tackle a workload; it's certainly admirable when somebody wants to do everything with excellence.

But it's a trap. Because if you do all the minor, non-crucial activities well, there are so many you'll find it nigh on impossible to get all of them done.

Even worse, it's common for many folks to get so caught up in the never-ending unimportant tasks that they run out of time to do the valuable ones. The result? Low levels of life achievement and high levels of life dissatisfaction.

Beware of this conundrum! And take an alternative path instead.

Rush unimportant tasks. Literally make a conscious decision that anything that is not particularly important you will do quickly, even if it means you do it averagely.

Now, many people cannot bring themselves to do this. They want to do everything beautifully. First, there's simply not enough time to do that and second, nobody cares if you do these things well—they just do not matter much.

As the world's greatest investor, Warren Buffett, so wisely put it: "What's not worth doing, is not worth doing well."

So what constitutes rushing? It's seems like a subjective concept. Well here's a good rule of thumb: most of the time, if you do a job to an 80 percent level, that is enough.

For example, let's say you're cleaning your desk. Cleaning it 80 percent well is usually quite sufficient. Or maybe you are writing an unimportant email to one of your company's suppliers. Doing it above an 80 percent level of quality is just not worth the loss of time.

You're far better off to move onto another unimportant task, or even better, an important one.

With this 80 percent method you will cross off far more from your To Do list. You'll feel a real sense of progress, of momentum. And believe me, nobody will even notice that you didn't do a perfect job on any of those trivial things. People just don't care.

Now of course, occasionally there are tasks that are relatively unimportant but must be done well. For example, you can't write a small check for someone and not complete it. But in the vast majority of cases, 80 percent is more than enough.

Now conversely, look at the effectiveness of the average (or below average) person.

We see them working long hours, and half the weekend, but at the end of the year they so often have not achieved all that much. How could this be possible? The answer could only be that they are either incompetent (not likely) or they're spending too long on stuff that is not really impactful to their success.

As the saying goes, they major in minor things.

So rush the unimportant. It clears your workload enormously and it gives you way more time for the few things in life that really matter.

WIN FAST ACTION STEPS

- Write a quick list of activities that you feel that you may spend too much time on.

- Experiment with rushing them – and when possible, not doing them at all.

- Once you've evaluated what tasks from the list can easily be rushed, refine your list down only to those tasks.

- Once you're happy that you are rushing what should be rushed, look to the people who work with you and see if together you can reduce their work times on unimportant jobs.

KNOW YOUR PERFECT DAY

You're about to read one of the most transformative techniques ever devised for personal and career success. It is a brilliant antidote to the all-too-common trap of working too hard for too few results.

It takes less than 15 minutes to do, but can positively affect your next 15 years.

The technique is called your perfect day.

Contemplate this. Most people say they want to have a fantastic day, but if you ask them what a fantastic day would look like, they can't immediately tell you! They have not thought about what their perfect day is. Now, you don't have to be a rocket scientist to realize that if you don't know what your perfect day is, your chances of achieving one consistently must be frighteningly small.

So mission one is to sit down for a few minutes and ask yourself this question: If I could design a perfect day for me, what would it actually look like?

Here's an example of one: up at 6 a.m. to enjoy a quiet

coffee and some serenity, while your favorite relaxing music plays in the background. Ten minutes of meditation followed by a 20-minute yoga session. Start work at 8:30 a.m. doing creative work and key projects uninterrupted until noon. Thirty minutes of emails followed by lunch with a great friend. Then an afternoon of meetings and calls with clients and staff, a short session of emails and finish work by 5:50 p.m. Dinner at 7 p.m. with friends or family, ending with a relaxing bath and then reading an award-winning book until bedtime at 10 p.m.

Now, that's just one of a million ways you could design your perfect day and your version may be completely different. The point is to actually design one, rather than do what 99.999 percent of society does, which is hope for wonderful days but do zero planning to orchestrate them.

As the old Chinese saying goes, "He who aims at nothing is sure to hit it."

Now, the reality is there will be many days that fall far short of perfect, and plenty of times when you will feel forced to tackle activities that you don't even like. But if you keep on aiming to create days like your perfect day, you will be delightfully surprised to find that sometimes you really do get to experience it, or pretty close to it. Certainly far more frequently than if you never even defined what a perfect day is to you.

Please keep in mind that you don't get what you want in life. Most of the time, you get what you carefully plan for and take consistent massive action towards.

WIN FAST ACTION STEPS

- In a few minutes, write out a first version of your perfect day.

- Remember that your initial perfect day doesn't have to be perfect; you will probably need to refine it over time.

- Make sure you explain the perfect day concept to those around you who could be impacted, and ask for their support.

- Each Sunday, review your upcoming week, looking for ways you can tailor each day to align with your perfect day.

CHANGE YOUR MOOD WITH YOUR POSTURE

Have you ever noticed that someone sad moves unlike someone happy?

Or that a person who is highly confident sits in a different way than somebody who is nervous?

The reason this occurs is that our body and our emotions are intimately linked. Almost all major moods are accompanied by particular physical movements or postures. So much so that we can often tell how someone is feeling merely by how they are standing, sitting or walking.

But what's really interesting about this is that it works the other way as well.

By changing our body's posture, we can significantly affect (and improve) our moods.

Imagine the implications of this! Used well, it could transform the quality of your entire life.

Let's say that you want to feel more confident. If you move your body for ten minutes as if you were highly confident, your confidence will actually increase.

If you want to feel calmer, you simply commit to moving

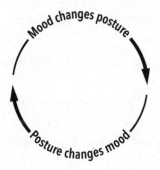

like you imagine a calm person would move, and sure enough, in just a few minutes you will indeed feel calmer.

If you are about to go into a really important meeting but you're feeling nervous about giving a presentation, you can simply spend some time moving as if you are a dynamic presenter and you are much more likely to present well.

It may seem absurd to you that you can alter your state (and your performance) just with your body movements, but you don't have to take my word for it. Try it yourself for ten minutes.

Choose a particular mood that you experience, then rank your degree of feeling about it out of ten.

For example, let us say that you are feeling lethargic. When considering just how tired you are, you give yourself a seven out of ten.

Then spend the next ten minutes moving as if you have a lot of energy: walking like someone with loads of energy, sitting like someone infused with energy, talking like someone totally energized, and using your hands like someone overflowing with energy.

Once you've done that, rank how tired you are now, out
of ten.

I can almost guarantee you will rank yourself more
energized.

Of course, the only way this works is if you fully commit
to behaving in the new way. If you do it in a half-hearted
manner, nothing will change. But if you do this experiment
full-on, you will definitely experience a rapid alteration in
your mood.

A tool like this can make a tangible improvement to how
well you perform over a lifetime. While other people behave
as if their moods control them, you will be one of an infinites-
imally small number of people who can actually be the master
of their moods.

That is real personal power.

WIN FAST ACTION STEPS

- Decide what someone with great confidence
  and energy would move like.
- Think about what someone who is empowered and
  charismatic would move like.
- Work out what someone calm, centered and strong
  would move like.
- In the next week try moving like each of these people
  for an hour and evaluate how that makes you feel
  and behave.

MAKE THE MOST
OF CAR TRAVEL

In a typical year, most of us spend hundreds of hours driving. Often alone.

It's a prime opportunity to do something to move our dreams forward, but most people waste that time daydreaming or just listening to the radio.

That's a real shame. There are so many alternative ways to maximize your driving time.

Here are four excellent ways you can turn driving time into a more productive pursuit:

1. Do Kegels while you drive.
Kegels are a fantastic exercise you can do at any time, without anyone knowing you're doing it. They are perfect to do while driving. To perform a Kegel, you just tense your pelvic muscles for 5 seconds, then relax for 3 seconds, then tense again for 5 seconds. (Your pelvic muscles are those muscles you feel when you stop urination in midstream.)

For women, the key benefit of doing Kegels is stronger bladder muscles, which can be weakened by pregnancy, childbirth or aging.

For men, Kegels also strengthen the bladder muscles, and according to the Mayo Clinic they may also improve sexual performance.

2. Listen to personal development, health or business podcasts.
Whenever I take my daughter to school, I use the return leg to listen to my favorite podcasts on the ten-minute trip back to home. Over the course of a year I learn a ton of stuff and arrive at my office inspired and raring to get into the day.

There are a colossal and ever-increasing number of great podcasts that can help you become a better person. Just press the podcast icon on your smartphone to access them.

3. Review your goals and how you're going with them.
Self-reflection is a lost art in today's fast-moving world. But driving your car alone is an ideal time to spend a few minutes to review what you are seeking to achieve in your life and evaluate your progress.

As the classical Greek philosopher Socrates once noted, "The unexamined life is not worth living." Using your commuting time to examine your life performance quickly refocuses you and pushes you to recommit to excellence.

4. *Update your gratitude list.*
Studies by the globally renowned psychologist Dr Martin Seligman have shown the significant power of thinking about what you are grateful for in your life. People who feel more grateful tend to have better health, better relationships and more overall happiness than the average person.

Each of these activities are easy to do and can be completed in a few minutes. Yet each of them can help you lead a more fulfilling life. Your vehicle really can be a vehicle for change.

WIN FAST ACTION STEPS

- Stick a reminder note in your car to use the time well.
- Jump into the podcasts section of your phone and look for topics that you'd like to learn about while you drive, then subscribe to a few.
- Try doing some Kegels next time you go for a drive.

FOLLOW A MORNING RITUAL

*The quality of your emotional state plays
a gigantic role in how successful you
will be in life.*

I'm sure you've experienced times when you started work in an agitated, bored or depressed mood. It's exceedingly hard to produce world-class work when you'd rather be in bed hiding under the covers.

Yet I'm sure you've also had times when you felt fabulous the moment you woke up. And as soon as you started work you were powerful, energized and loving life.

Same person, completely different level of enjoyment and results.

So why the huge variance in mood? Why do we start some days in a foul, uninspired mood and others feeling better than awesome? It's quite a mystery, and it may be many years before researchers solve it, but what we do know is that there are several things you can do to massively increase the chances that you'll feel good in the morning—and consequently perform better throughout the day.

The best method I know of is the morning ritual.

Instead of just waking up and doing the same old stuff you normally do, imagine if you set a routine that virtually guarantees you went out into the world feeling fantastic. That's what a good morning ritual can give you.

You get to design your own morning ritual and determine its length. Some people do a ritual that's only five minutes long, whereas others take much longer. My usual current ritual is around fifty minutes and it's part of every morning, Monday to Friday.

Here's a list of cool things you can insert into your personal morning ritual:

Prayer.

Gratitude list.

Review your goals.

A quick walk or run.

Watch a TED talk.

Ten deep breaths.

Three minutes of stretching.

Visualize performing well that day.

Say positive focusing statements.

Listen to uplifting music.

Read a motivating book for

  ten minutes.

Pick whatever you want, but choose activities that you find relatively easy, enjoyable and uplifting. You should feel good about doing your morning ritual, not dread it, so choose what interests you the most.

However you design it, to start your day with an organized, soul-nurturing morning ritual really is one of the most potent tools for taking your life to a far higher level.

Make it a central part of your life and "Good morning" won't just be something you say, it'll be something you experience every day.

WIN FAST ACTION STEPS

- Design a ten-minute morning ritual that you can comfortably do even if you're busy.
- Consider what else you could include if you extended your morning ritual to thirty minutes.
- Start the morning ritual experiment with a ten-minute version.

LEARN FROM THE TERRIBLE PERFORMERS AROUND YOU

As you stretch yourself to be excellent, you will quickly notice how few people around you are striving to be above average in any substantial way.

Most people are content with the status quo and never consistently push themselves to be extraordinary in their work or their life.

That of course is good news for you, as your competition is infinitely smaller because of the generally lackadaisical attitude of the masses.

Most people would counsel you to ignore these people but I take a contrary view—I think they can be a major source of your future success. Every person you regularly interact with is a huge reservoir of opportunity for you, if you learn to observe them very carefully. And then do the exact opposite.

That's right, I want you to watch mediocre people very carefully and regularly set aside some time to ask yourself what exactly makes them perform so averagely?

Think about someone you work with currently, somebody whom everyone around them thinks poorly of. Why is that happening?

What are they doing that gives such a poor impression? How are they behaving to be losing the respect and confidence of many of the people they interact with?

Is it that they are rude? Or lazy? Do they not deliver on what they promise, or is it their arrogance that agitates people who deal with them?

Maybe it's their listening skills that are letting them down. It could be their sloppy personal presentation that gives such a bad impression.

Usually it will be a combination of three to five different aspects that together make the majority of people who have much to do with them dislike the experience.

So think about some of their character traits and write them down. Then set yourself the goal of becoming the exact opposite of what they are. Few people ever study the mediocre; instead they only look at the top performers. I think that's a mistake, because there are ten times more people who perform badly than perform well, so there's a lot more opportunity to learn from the mediocre folks than from superlative ones.

Yet the lessons of terrible performers are every bit as useful as the lessons gleaned from the elite achievers—if only you take the time to study them.

Here's an interesting concept to think about: To be successful in life, you don't have to be particularly amazing, you just need to not make major errors, for an extended period of time. If you can go through the next twenty years not doing what people who get bad results have done, ipso facto you will end up doing very well indeed.

The ultra achievers in life are not just playing a defensive game, they're going for victory by making a series of positive proactive moves and devising strategies to win fast, but concurrently they are deeply aware of the flaws of average performers and work hard not to emulate them.

You must do the same.

To avoid being bad you must clearly know what being bad looks like in your field or situation. It may seem like a Zen koan or riddle, but winners do not just win, they avoid losing.

WIN FAST ACTION STEPS

- Identify three people you know who are not doing well, in life or at work.

- Think about why that's the case and see if you can identify three flaws in how each of them think or behave.

- Now compare their situation with yours. How could you act in the exact opposite way to them?

- Are there any ways that you are actually similar to them?

HAVE A WEEKLY ADMIN DAY

Life is messy. Sometimes really messy.

And if we don't regularly clean things up, the mess grows like a giant weed and takes over both our physical environment and our mind.

What kind of mess am I talking about? In the environmental category, I include cleaning your desk and office. Paying bills. Processing mail. Organizing documents. Emptying in-trays. Doing your filing. Storing stuff. Keeping up-to-date with all emails. Throwing out surplus paraphernalia.

Then there's the mental category. In this I include getting clear on your goals. Getting your To Do lists totally up-to-date. Personal education (doing online courses, reading books and attending seminars). Clarifying what you value in life. Generally getting clear and present as to who you are and what you are trying to do in life.

When you clean up both your environmental and your mental messes, you feel really good inside. You feel in control and on top of things, externally and internally.

There are two ways you can reach this exalted state.

You can do a little bit of it every day, or you can save it all up and get it done once a week.

Mon	Tues	Wed	Thur	Fri
Work	Work	Work	Admin	Work

The trouble with doing some administration every day (as it comes in) is that you often end up almost constantly spending time on these little tasks and, if you're not careful, your day can become almost filled with admin jobs.

That's why I'm a fan of setting a half day or full day aside each week and getting all these little jobs and messes done in one big session. For me, it's usually each Friday morning for three hours.

When a new piece of paperwork or admin comes in, unless you can deal with it in a couple of minutes I suggest you just file it away, knowing that you'll get to it during your weekly admin session.

The beauty of this technique is that your week becomes much simpler and easier to manage. At least 80 percent of your week you are working on the tasks that really matter. Then for one half day or one full day you are tending to all the other admin tasks. In one fell swoop.

It's a far neater way to structure your week.

Now there's only one danger with confining all your admin to one day. You must actually deal with it when you say you will!

If you set up a weekly admin day and then avoid doing it for two or three weeks in a row, chaos soon ensues. You must, must, *must* do your weekly admin session each and every week. Put it into your calendar and don't let anything get in the way of completing it.

Even if you have other work on your plate. Even if a client wants to meet with you that day. Even if you don't particularly feel like it.

It takes a little practice to make the admin day a habit, but once you do you'll never return to processing admin on a rolling basis. Your weeks will feel so much smoother and easier when you don't have to stop every hour or so to get the small stuff done. And the time available to spend on your more important tasks will grow enormously.

WIN FAST ACTION STEPS

- Pick one day of the week as your admin day.
- Block out that day in your calendar.
- Create a list of standard tasks that you will handle on that day.
- Strongly resist letting anything prevent your admin day from happening, but if you do have to forgo your admin day, then set up a new one as soon as possible. Don't wait for the following week's admin day.

MAKE THE MOST IMPORTANT CHOICE IN THE WORLD

Although I probably don't know you,
I know quite a lot about you.

Because you bought this book, I know that you are striving for excellence. I know you have a kind of inspired dissatisfaction with your life as it is. You want to achieve more, earn more and be more.

This is not just a positive thing, it is a natural one. All of nature strives to make the most of its life. Even the smallest flower strives valiantly to reach for the sun.

But be careful. Your desire to better your situation is in my view a noble one, but make sure it doesn't make you feel that you are not enough just as you are.

It's a subtle distinction. There is a small difference between someone who works to succeed for the challenge, adventure and rewards of it, versus a person who is just as motivated but is doing it because they think it will make them happy. That they have a piece missing that only success will fill.

If that sounds like you, then you need to know the truth. Happiness is not a matter of improving your material circumstances. There are huge bodies of research that show that once a person has their basic needs met, increased income has only a small effect on someone's happiness. (And even that usually dissipates over time.)

A while ago, I was sitting next to a friend at dinner whose brother is one of the richest people on the planet. A multi-billionaire. The guy told me this brother was also a deeply miserable man. To be honest, that didn't surprise me. When I wrote two books on happiness, there was one research study that made a huge impression on me.

Renowned happiness researcher Ed Diener tested 49 of the Forbes 400 richest people in America. They showed on average only 1 percent higher happiness than the average American wage earner.

The truth is, being happy is largely a choice. A choice to say to yourself, "I am going to choose to be happy today, no matter what happens. I am going to choose to really enjoy my life, regardless of whether I feel I won or lost on that particular day, week or year.

"I choose not to be a puppet to my circumstances, feeling down when things go poorly and elated when things go well. Instead I choose to be the maker of my own joy, to be far more mighty than anything that may happen in my environment. I choose to be happy right now."

This really is the greatest choice you can make in the world. And I truly hope you make it.

WIN FAST ACTION STEPS

- Make the commitment right now to choose to be happy regardless of your circumstances.

- Write the letter "H" on some small pieces of paper and place them in various places in your office and home to remind you to stick to this philosophy.

- Teach this concept to somebody you care about.

CENTER YOURSELF BEFORE EVERY MEETING

Here's a super-quick technique that will dramatically improve your performance in any interaction you have with others – business or personal.

Just before you walk into the room where you are meeting people, spend a few moments calming yourself and centering your mind. Get yourself relaxed and present in the moment.

It's so important to do this. So often we walk into our next meeting carrying the stress or bad feelings from whatever we were doing just beforehand.

Maybe you have just had a bad phone call, or an argument with someone. Perhaps you were brooding about something negative in your life, or worrying about a dear friend's problems. If you are not careful, you will bring that disempowered mindset into your next meeting and it can have negative and, in some cases, disastrous effects.

You may end up snapping at people who really don't deserve it, or presenting poorly because your mind is not fully focused on the here and now. Or simply not being the sharp, vibrant, positive force for good that you aspire to be.

We're all human, of course, so at times even the most evolved and professional person will come into a meeting carrying negative mental baggage from an earlier moment or frame of mind. But with ultrasuccessful people, these times are exceedingly rare; whereas with mediocre people it happens very often. You will enjoy better outcomes if you reduce to zero the times you enter a meeting upset or frazzled. This is true for both your personal and your business life.

You can get centered several ways.

Taking three deep breaths works well. Staring at an object for a few seconds is effective, too. Some sports-performance experts recommend loosening your lower jaw by moving it around a little to de-stress. Others recommend saying a few positive, encouraging words to yourself.

Or try the famous Buddhist mind-centering technique. It involves quietly focusing your mind on the inflow and outflow of your breath.

Try a few of these centering methods and then settle on one or two that really resonate with you. Then whenever you are moving from one human interaction to another, take a few moments to get yourself focused and resettled.

When you are agitated, you will almost always perform below your best. But when you are truly centered you can amaze the world.

WIN FAST ACTION STEPS

- Give each of the centering techniques a try to see which you feel most comfortable with.
- Think of another way you could settle yourself.
- Consider inserting one of these centering techniques into your daily morning ritual.

USE SLEEP AS A WEAPON

For decades, many hard-driving, success-oriented people have taken pride in how little sleep they need. I've read more than one article where a prominent CEO will boast about only needing four hours a night, implying that it makes them more powerful than the average person who needs more.

But in the last few years, a wave of new research has shown that these people are being very foolish if they think they're achieving superior performance by sleeping less. The opposite is in fact true.

The new evidence is clear that getting more and better-quality sleep is one of the best weapons for you to beat your competitors. Studies show that if you get a good snooze of at least seven to eight hours a night, you will think better, have more energy, be more optimistic, be less cranky, process information more effectively, remember more, have greater willpower, be physically stronger, age slower, have a stronger sex drive and get much more done.

What an impressive list. Seriously, can you think of any other activity that can credibly offer as many benefits?

So yes, duration of sleep is very important. But so is the quality of sleep.

To maximize this, the studies show that you should sleep in a totally dark room, as darkness will increase your production of melatonin, the master cell-repair hormone.

You should sleep away from devices with electrical fields, such as cell phones, power cords and electric clocks.

You should keep your room as quiet as possible and keep the room temperature on the cool side—15.5–19.5°C (60–67°F) is optimum. (You'll not only sleep better but you'll burn more calories, too.)

Additionally, you should not be staring at a computer or phone screen within an hour of your sleep time, as it will stimulate your senses when they should be quieting down and make it much harder to drop off to sleep.

So, as you can see, there's quite a science to maximizing your sleep, a science that most of your competitors don't know about and won't make the most of. When you think about it, it's a great opportunity to not just increase your health and happiness, but also perform at a higher level than your peers.

That's why so many prominent leaders are very focused on a sleep routine that prioritizes high quality and beneficial length. An example comes from one of the world's richest men, Jeff Bezos. Here's what he says about the importance of sleep and how it affects decision making:

> Eight hours of sleep makes a big difference for me and
> I try hard to make that a priority . . . If you short-change

your sleep you might get a couple of "extra-productive" hours, but that productivity might be an illusion.

Clearly, in today's competitive environment, plentiful sleep isn't just nice to have. It's an absolute must.

WIN FAST ACTION STEPS

- Mentally commit to practicing sleep excellence from now on.
- Consider setting an alarm at, say, 9 p.m. to remind you it's time to start preparing for bed.
- Set up a chair or table at least 1 meter away from your bed to put your electric alarm clock and phone on, so they are away from your body.

RUTHLESSLY UNSUBSCRIBE

When asked the secret to success, the legendary effectiveness expert Stephen Covey answered: "The main thing is to keep the main thing the main thing."

In other words, you must relentlessly focus on your primary objectives and not be curtailed by interruptions and sidetracks.

Easy to say, but so hard to do. Particularly in the age of the internet. Seemingly almost every second we are interrupted by another social post, YouTube video, podcast or email newsletter. Each one tempting us to stop what we are doing and click them to see what they're about.

These days it really takes iron willpower to resist some of these distractions, but resist you must. Because each may only take you away from your life's work for a few minutes, but together they can end up wasting weeks of your time over the course of the year, while radically reducing your concentration and productivity.

There are defensive actions you can take that will help a lot. Turn off that option on your computer that notifies you of a new email. Delete any automated communications and

Reduction adds to your life

texts from Facebook, Instagram, Snapchat or LinkedIn. Close your email when you are not actively using it.

Perhaps the most important tactic is to ruthlessly unsubscribe from all but the most valued digital messages.

All those apps you downloaded? Unsubscribe from 90 percent of them.

All those email newsletters you opted in for? Opt out from all but the most important.

All those push notifications that interrupt you twenty times a day? Get rid of them, pronto.

These things are stealing your focus and attention, two of the most crucial ingredients for your potential success. Unsubscribe, unsubscribe, unsubscribe.

Yes, you will have withdrawal symptoms at first, but a week or two later you will have adapted to life without them—and soon be enjoying a true rarity in today's hyper-commented world: peace. Serenity of both mind and environment. Your calm will rise and your productivity will soar.

There is no chance in a million years that you can achieve great things while being constantly interrupted by incessant digital chatter. A scattered mind produces weak outcomes.

Remember what most of these interruptions actually are—messages sent from companies and celebrities that want to make money from you, via advertising or promotions.

These are people trying to fulfill their own dreams by seducing you to stop working on yours to pay attention to theirs.

Unsubscribe from them ruthlessly and take back control of your time, your focus and your future. Opting out of them is opting in to achieving more, earning more and being more.

WIN FAST ACTION STEPS

- When you review your morning emails from companies, specifically look for regular ones that come in that you could unsubscribe to.

- Review the apps on your phone and delete as many as possible. If you think you might need some one day, remember that you can always upload them again.

- Review which YouTube subscriptions, Twitter feeds and social-media influencers you should unfollow.

READ BOOKS IN ONE HOUR

If we are in the Information Age, then surely one of the most important skills is to read information quickly.

Often the only reason that someone rises higher in their profession is simply because they learned a few more valuable things than everyone else, then applied them. Where did they get this learning? Often from books, reports, websites, specialist blogs or the print media. In short, the written word.

So if information is power, then it would certainly pay to be able to digest a lot of information in very little time.

Hence my speed-reading technique for books.

Here's the gist of it. The next time you have a nonfiction book to read (it could be personal development, business, a trade book or health-related), give yourself just 60 minutes to read it.

(Merely setting that deadline alone should speed things up quite a bit.)

First, read the inside flaps and the back cover.

Then scan the table of contents so that you know the essence of what the author is going to talk about.

Next, quickly read the introduction and the conclusion or final chapter. This is usually where the core concepts and nuggets of wisdom will be summarized. (Frankly, with many nonfiction books you could just stop there, and you'd already have covered the author's key points.)

Finally, we get to the main body of the book.

Now the trick here is to just read the first sentence of each paragraph. The way most nonfiction books are structured, I've found that, in general, most of the key points are introduced at the beginning of a paragraph, so often you don't have to read the rest of that paragraph. Just move on to the first line of the next paragraph, and so on, until you've got through each chapter.

The only part of each chapter you should read in full is the very last paragraph. That's because it's always where the author sums up the most salient points of that section.

Voilà. You can now read a book in about an hour.

One final tip about getting the most out of books in a short period of time: Make it your aim to only seek three big ideas from a book, rather than aiming to walk away with a mountain of concepts.

Paradoxically, getting a whole lot of ideas often proves almost useless, as you usually end up not acting on any of them. By focusing on gleaning the three best ones and then acting on them, you are much more likely to use the author's wisdom to actually improve your life.

The right book can change your life. The problem is that many people think that books are too long and so don't even attempt to read them. This technique allows you to capture the very best ideas from books, without having to spend hours laboriously wading through every word of them, just to find a handful of gems.

WIN FAST ACTION STEPS

- Pick a simple book to trial this technique.
- Set an alarm to keep you on track with how much time you spend reading.
- Remember you don't have to read the book in a single one-hour sitting; three sessions of 20 minutes can be ideal and less challenging.

DO YOUR MOST IMPORTANT TASKS FIRST

I have spent literally thousands of hours studying time management and productivity.

I've tested hundreds of different techniques to see what were the most effective for helping people achieve more.

Some of these productivity methods are pretty out-there and some are quite complex. But when it comes down to it, I fervently believe that if you could only implement one single technique to send your productivity results through the roof, it would be a really, really simple one.

Do your most important tasks first.

Let me tell you a story.

In 1918 there was a great industrialist by the name of Charles M. Schwab. Founder of the Bethlehem Steel Corporation, the second-biggest steel producer in the U.S. at that time, Schwab was one of the richest men in the world.

One day he had a conversation with another businessman by the name of Ivy Lee about his desire to make his executives much more productive. Lee said he would train Schwab's executives with a special technique, then after three months

Schwab could choose what to pay Lee, based on the results of his executives using the technique.

The technique, in essence, was to do the most important tasks first.

In detail, the system was as follows:

Every evening, write down the six most important tasks you have to do the next day. No more than six. Prioritize them 1–6 in order of importance.

When you get to work the following day, start doing number one on the list and do not begin any others until you have completed number one. Only then do you move on to number two etc.

How valuable was this technique for Charles Schwab and the Bethlehem Steel Corporation executives?

Three months later Schwab gave Ivy Lee a check for $25,000. That, ladies and gentlemen, would be worth more than $400,000 in today's money.

That's how effective the technique was.

At the heart of it, most ambitious people make a critical mistake when it comes to their productivity. They think it's about getting more tasks done. In fact, it's about getting the *most valuable* tasks done. There is a gigantic difference between the two.

Don't get me wrong. Getting a lot done is fabulous. But it won't get you to the top. Only consistently doing the right tasks will do that.

Now here's the irony: It is often because we are desperately trying to get more done that we fail to identify the handful of tasks that really matter. Our focus on quantity-based productivity actually reduces our quality-based productivity.

It can be quite confronting to face this in your own life. The cold fact is that if you have been working long hours without great success, it's probably because your productivity focus has been quantity-based.

The fantastic news is that you only need a small amount of time each day to identify what's really important and obsessively do these tasks first. And this huge problem will be solved.

WIN FAST ACTION STEPS

- Try the Schwab technique tomorrow morning.
- In rare cases you'll find that you won't be able to complete a task because you are waiting for someone else's work or more information. In that case, move on to the next task, but return to the previous one as soon as you finish what you're working on.
- Resist the urge to put more than six tasks on your list each day. Stick to the system.

HEAT AND COOL YOUR BRAIN

If you want to be more successful than the people around you, it pays to look where your competitors aren't.

In that vein, one of the most fruitful areas to study at the moment is brainpower maximization. It's a hot subject because in the last ten years there's been a huge increase in the number of discoveries about how to improve our brain function.

Obviously, our performance in life is intricately connected to how well we use our brain.

After all, it's the instrument of every action we take and every thought we have. So surely anything we can do to improve our brain's performance is going to be incredibly valuable.

One such way is to work in a warmer environment.

Cornell University conducted a fascinating study where they tested executive performance at a major Florida insurance company. When temperatures were a low 20°C (68°F) the company's staff made 44 percent more mistakes compared to when the room was a normal temperature (25°C/77°F).

Forty-four percent more mistakes! That is an enormous difference, I'm sure you'll agree.

One of the reasons that cold working environments are not as effective as warm ones is that when it's cold the body is forced to devote more of its energy resources to keeping the body warm. If it's doing this for between eight and ten hours a day, that is a significant diversion of the body's energy away from the brain, where it's most needed.

Interestingly, the Cornell study showed that not only do people think better in a warmer environment, they seem to be happier as well.

Now what is somewhat perplexing is that when it comes to getting a sound night's sleep, the opposite is true. Most people sleep much better in a cool environment.

How cool? Between 15.5 and 19.5°C (60 and 67°F) is ideal, according to several studies.

Indeed, a University of South Australia study showed that sleeping in a colder room reported a reduced rate of insomnia. Other studies show an increase in melatonin and human growth hormone production when people slept in cooler environments, both crucial for the body's repair systems. Other studies suggest that you can even lose more weight when you slumber in a colder room.

Remarkable findings. Clearly your brain is highly sensitive to temperature variations, so to optimize your performance ensure that you keep your environment warmer during the day and cooler overnight.

WIN FAST ACTION STEPS

- If you work for somebody else, explain the science behind temperature and performance and ask them to approve a trial of working in a warmer climate. Before this occurs, brief your team members about the benefits.

- At home, experiment with the colder sleep temperature for at least two days, as it can take some getting used to.

FOLLOW THE
TWO-MINUTE RULE

Sick of endless To-Do lists? Tired of the avalanche of emails? Stressed every time you look at your desk, your garage or your files?

You need the Two-Minute Rule.

It's so, so simple, yet so strikingly effective for anybody who is feeling exasperated by the sheer volume of stuff that threatens to overwhelm their everyday life.

If that pretty much sums up your predicament, then here's what you need to do. Institute the simple rule that every time a new task comes up you ask yourself one powerful question:

"Can I do this in two minutes or less?"

If the answer is yes, you must do it immediately. If the answer is no, it would take longer than two minutes, then the task goes on your To-Do list for later.

Oh what a difference this elementary method makes! You see, half the reason you probably feel overwhelmed by your life is the sheer volume of things you have to do. This endless mountain of demands eats away at you day and night, keeping your baseline of stress dangerously high. But I bet that when

?

Key question: What can you do in two minutes?

you analyze that gargantuan list you will see a decent chunk of the items on it, maybe 20 or 30 percent, could be done very quickly—usually within two minutes.

Answering that email. Calling that person. Booking that restaurant. Saying no or yes to a request. Cleaning up your desk. Clarifying your next most important task to tackle. These are all quick tasks to complete, but so often we don't address them as soon as they come in, so, like the Sorcerer's Apprentice in Disney's *Fantasia*, the water keeps rising on us until we feel like we're about to be drowned.

It's way better to tackle the jobs as soon as they come in, as long as they can be done in two minutes or less.

The advantages of working this way are numerous.

Your To-Do list decreases massively in size. You feel real momentum because you're getting lots of stuff done each day. Your confidence increases as you start to take control of your tasks, rather than letting them pile up.

When I coach executives on getting their workload under control, time and time again they say the Two-Minute Rule helps them enormously.

Got two minutes right now? Give it a try.

SIIMON REYNOLDS

WIN FAST ACTION STEPS

- When you have multiple minor tasks, pick the most valuable one to do first.
- If you find that one of them is starting to take much longer than two minutes, stop doing it for now and write it on your To-Do list.

STOP SEEKING EASE
AND CALM

*There are two fundamental ways to see the world
and our place in it.*

The first is that we should get up in the morning in order to strive for and experience the good things in life: pleasurable moments, objects and experiences.

People with this frame of mind have a central vision of their lives as potentially blissful . . . if they can just get over the unpleasant hardships and troubles that burden them now.

But this mode of thought has a downside. If not kept in check, it can become an endless search for pleasure and good times. As soon as we achieve a pleasant moment or experience, we can't fully appreciate it, because the urge to seek our next hit of bliss is too strong.

This attitude is very common. In fact, there's actually a term for it in psychology—the hedonic treadmill—that clearly implies that those walking this path are endlessly chasing pleasures in the future while not being able to enjoy the present good times or progress in any meaningful way.

The alternative way to see the world has challenge at its core, rather than pleasure.

This group of people proactively seek the obstacles and the struggle, and love the thrill and satisfaction of overcoming them.

Of course, they like the good times as well, but importantly, pleasure is not their *primary* driver, just a nice by-product of it.

I believe that one of the most powerful shifts you can make is to stop seeking ease and calm, and choose to live your life by the second paradigm.

And even go further. I recommend that you begin thinking of yourself as someone who actually loves the fight, who seeks tough times, who is comfortable being uncomfortable, who experiences hardship on the way to their goal and says, "Bring it on!"

Taking on this kind of self-identity doesn't eliminate any hardship in your life, but it sure as hell reduces the impact of it.

When you choose to see yourself as unstoppable, you are not at all perturbed when things turn difficult. In fact, you expect it. You see difficulties as normal and customary to living an interesting life, rather than something to be feared and avoided, or a sign that something is terribly wrong.

There are tribes of people in the world who definitely think this way. One interesting example is the elite military unit the U.S. Navy SEALs. I have studied their training methods in depth and found how they deliberately seek to install an ambivalent or even welcoming attitude towards challenging situations.

To the point where the motto of the Navy SEALs is: "The only easy day was yesterday."

How much more potent an attitude like this is than seeing hardship as something to be avoided at all costs.

One thing we know is this: Life is going to keep throwing hard times at us, whether we like it or not. So it makes a lot of sense to choose to shape your self-identify as someone who is totally cool with this state of affairs.

WIN FAST ACTION STEPS

- Each time you look at yourself in the mirror, take a moment to look into your eyes and think to yourself, "I'm unstoppable! Bring it on!" This will help a lot to remodel your self-image to fit this new way of thinking.
- The next time you are facing a difficulty, reflect on how you felt when you were last in front of a mirror.
- Place a note in your wallet that says, "The tougher it gets, the better I get."

CLEAR YOUR MIND
EACH EVENING

Here's a technique that will make you both more successful and give you peace of mind.

I call it the Evening Mind Clearance.

At the end of a stressful day, many people find themselves tossing and turning in bed, worrying about their life. This ruminating about what happened in the daylight hours rarely improves your situation, majorly increases stress and greatly reduces actual sleep time.

It's an awful way to end the day.

But start doing the Evening Mind Clearance and everything will change for the better.

In essence, the mind clearance has three steps.

First, you create a list of the things that you're grateful for in your life.

All too often, we forget all the good stuff that happens in a typical day and instead end up focusing on the one or two things that went wrong. By simply creating a mental list of the positive parts of the day that you're grateful for, your mood is almost instantly lifted and your mind becomes much more serene.

The second step is to forgive anyone who has behaved badly towards you.

Perhaps a workmate was rude to you, or a friend was disrespectful. Think about each of these such moments and instead of replaying the scene over and over and getting more and more worked up, just send them forgiveness and kind thoughts and let it all go.

I've heard a Chinese parable in which two monks were forbidden to touch women. One day they were walking out in the countryside and they encountered a young lady who could not cross a river. One of the monks offered to help her across the water and she thankfully agreed. He picked her up, waded across the river and put her down safely on the other side.

For the next three hours, the other monk refused to talk to the first monk, so upset was he that his friend had broken the monastic rules.

Finally, the monk who helped the woman turned to him and said, "I put that woman down three hours ago. Why are you still carrying her?"

If you have a grievance with someone, each night simply forgive them as much as you can, and let it go. Believe me, your life will be a whole lot happier if you do.

Just taking the first two steps will vastly lower your evening stress levels, but taking one more step moves you to an even better mental place.

In the third step you spend just a minute or two before sleep visualizing the next day and your life in general going really well. See yourself performing superbly, imagine yourself enjoying the day and feeling great about what you've achieved at the end of it.

No matter what stress you've experienced throughout that day, this visualization switches your mind back to you living an inspiring and optimistic future.

Doing the Evening Mind Clearance will take you only three to five minutes, but it will clear your mind of much of your day's stress and agitation, replacing worry with calm and anxiety with positivity.

WIN FAST ACTION STEPS

- With the third step (imagining the next day going well), how you feel is as important as the pictures you see in your mind. Try to really *feel* that the upcoming day you're imagining is successful, that you'll do a superb job, that you are optimistic and energized.

- A good time to do the Evening Mind Clearance is when you first lie down in bed, before you get too sleepy.

USE THE SCIENCE OF LUCK

*Do you believe in luck? Surprisingly,
I've found that the majority of people do.*

At the very least, I think you'll agree that there certainly seem to be times when good situations arise that are statistically extremely improbable.

For instance, you decide to open a business and that very night you meet a person who needs exactly what you're selling. Or you need an answer to an important question and you happen to open a book and there it is. When you think about the low probability of moments like that, it boggles the mind.

There are two main theories about luck, and I think both of them are true.

The first is that when you think intensely about something, the universe sometimes brings it to you. As absurd as this hypothesis appears at first, a little bit of research on magnetic fields and basic quantum physics suggests that your thoughts can indeed manifest your reality.

The second main theory about luck is that it is a science and that if you do certain things you will become luckier.

In my view the leader in this field is Professor Richard Wiseman. (If you're going to be a professor, how lucky are you to be born with the surname Wiseman?!)

Wiseman has studied both good and bad luck in depth with laboratory experiments, intensive interviewing of people perceived to be lucky and numerous psychometric questionnaires.

His conclusion is that you can become much luckier if you follow four basic principles:

1. You maximize chance opportunities. Lucky people create a lot more opportunity for luck to happen, by going out and interacting with people, reaching out to companies, and maintaining a network of friends and associates that could help them. Then when an opportunity arises, they take action and make the most of the chance.
2. You listen to lucky hunches. Professor Wiseman found that lucky people tend to trust their intuition. When many people would ignore a feeling inside about taking a certain risk, people who experience more luck are more likely to act on those hunches.
3. You expect good fortune. Lucky people deeply believe that their future is going to be full of good fortune. This becomes a self-fulfilling prophecy, as they persist when times are bad and always act positively when interacting with others.

4. You attempt to turn your bad luck into good.
   Lucky people are far more likely to believe that
   unfortunate events that happen in their life will
   turn out to be good in the end. They also don't
   dwell on misfortune and, equally importantly, they
   take constructive steps to improve any adverse
   situation, hence reversing their original bad luck.

What I love about Richard's research is that it's so actionable.
Right now you can decide to follow these four principles,
and you'll become much luckier for the rest of your life. How
wonderful is that?

WIN FAST ACTION STEPS

- Start with luck-increasing principle number one.
- Who could you reconnect with? What upcoming events
could you attend or even initiate so that you are increasing
the chances of lucky interactions by colliding with other
people who could help you achieve your goals?

GET SUPER CLEAR ABOUT WHAT YOU WANT

Arguably the most crucial component of success is not intelligence. It's clarity about what you want in life and how you're going to get it.

As the great personal-achievement guru Brian Tracy says, "An average person will run rings around a genius, if that person is clear about their goals and the genius isn't." How true that is.

Yet bizarrely, in my experience very few people can answer the question "What are your goals?" with an immediate, cogent and definite response.

Oh sure, most people have some vague concept of where they'd like to go, but they lack definiteness and precision of thought. In the 1930s, Napoleon Hill famously interviewed many of America's most successful people and concluded that definiteness of purpose was the most important factor of all when it came to high achievement.

Most people are in a fog of doubt and confusion about what they want. This makes it virtually impossible for them to fulfill their potential or even choose good next steps to improve their lives.

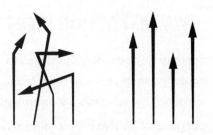

Clarity of direction is crucial

Clarity really is power. So here are six incredibly important questions to get clear on if you want to achieve at a high level. I call them the Super Six:

1. Where do I want to be in one, three and ten years?
2. Why is it vital that I achieve these goals?
3. What are the best steps to get me there?
4. By what date could I get each of those steps done?
5. What are the potential obstacles that could stop me achieving these goals?
6. What could I do to overcome or avoid those obstacles?

The Super Six are insanely powerful, yet there wouldn't be one person in a hundred who has answered all of them. Which explains why so few people achieve at a high level.

Get clear on the Super Six and you'll get clear on what you want in life. It will immediately improve your chances of success in any area of life you want to focus on.

WIN FAST ACTION STEPS

- Answer the six questions, then spend a day or two regularly coming back to them to see if they are what you want to *truly* commit to.

- Read your goals at least every morning, to focus your mind for the day.

- Consider reading your goals several times a day (see page 7).

- Whenever you have a spare moment, ask yourself what is one thing you could do immediately to get you closer to those goals.

CREATE A SET OF
FIVE LIFE RULES

*Unfortunately, life doesn't come with an
instruction manual.*

So we have no choice but to formulate our own set of instructions or guidelines for living well, to make the most of our time on this planet.

Yet in my experience, not even one person in a hundred has a clear set of rules about how they wish to lead their life. As a result of this lack of clarity, the average person can be very indecisive about which choices to make, who to befriend, what goals to pursue and how to design a life that brings them as much joy and as little sorrow as possible.

With no firm directional rudder, their ship of life changes direction with the ever-changing prevailing winds.

As the saying goes, "If you don't stand for something, you'll fall for anything."

There's a simple and elegant solution, though. Take some time to develop a short set of rules that you do your very best to follow throughout your life.

Keep the list short. Five is a good number, but it could be three or six. The main thing is to keep your life guidelines brief enough that you remember them and actually embed them into your life. A list of, say, fifteen life rules is hard to even recall, let alone apply consistently.

And understand that when you create these rules, you'll try very hard to stick to them, but recognize that there will always be times when you'll falter or need to be flexible. Just cut yourself some slack when that happens.

What are some good examples of life rules? Here are a few to get your mind thinking.

Bring fun into every day.	*Health before wealth.*	*Think big*
Choose to forgive.	*Do everything with excellence.*	*Don't take life too seriously.*
Let go.		*Be the leader.*
Say yes to adventure.	*Be light and strong.*	*Do your best and move on.*
God first.	*Expansion always.*	
Be grateful.	*Go the extra mile.*	*I am always clear about my goals.*
Leave everything better than you found it.	*I do what I say I will.*	

This kind of thing. Remember, there are no "right" answers here; whatever resonates with you as good principles to live your life by are fine. These rules are not for others to judge—in fact you may well never show them to another soul. These are for your edification and use only.

A sure sign that you have chosen a good set of rules is that when you finish coming up with them, you feel both clear and inspired. You should feel, "Yes! This is how I want to live my life."

Don't expect to create a perfect list on your first go at it. You will almost certainly want to refine the initial list as you test your principles in the cauldron of life.

But at least now you will have direction, inspiration and the confidence that you aren't just meandering through life, but are in fact one of the very few who live with clarity, standards and purpose.

WIN FAST ACTION STEPS

- Do a 24-hour test of this method.
- Create a quick list of five life rules you could potentially live by, then focus on following them and behaving accordingly for the entire one-day period.
- Note how you perform and how you feel, then adjust your list based on your results.

CREATE GREAT PLANS
IN TEN MINUTES

At the heart of achieving great things is a well-designed framework of carefully considered plans.

If you do no planning and just wing it, what you achieve in life is in the lap of the gods.

If you do poor planning, sometimes you'll get an okay result, but plenty of times you'll experience a whole lot of pain and failure.

But if you learn to plan effectively, you will at least double your chances of success at anything you try.

That being the case, it amazes me how few people learn how to plan well. It's not even that hard, you just need a good framework to work with.

Here is that framework.

It's known as PROP, and it's an exceedingly simple but effective rapid-planning tool. Using the PROP methodology, if you concentrate, you can often create excellent plans for any goal you want to pursue in ten minutes or less.

Here are the four steps of the PROP process.

1. *Define Priorities.* What are the most important
   priorities for your goal?
2. *Identify Realities.* What is the raw truth of the situation
   and how does that affect your options?
3. *Create Options.* What options do you have to move
   towards your goal?
4. *Design the Path.* Based on all this information, what
   should your plan be and in what order should the
   steps of the plan be taken?

Deploying the PROP sequence on all your major goals ensures that you are not cutting corners with your planning. The two elements of PROP that are most useful for me are steps 2 and 3.

Often people create plans that at first look good, but upon further reflection are unrealistic, because some factors have been overlooked. Step 2 ensures that you address such factors early in the project, rather than having your goal scuttled by them later.

Step 3, *creating options*, is vital too. Please note that it is Option*s* plural. This forces you not to just settle on the first plan that pops into your head. For every goal, you need to brainstorm multiple solutions, to increase certainty that you're choosing the very best path forward available.

Now that you have the PROP framework to work with, planning can easily become more thorough, even as it becomes quicker to accomplish.

By simply spending a few minutes on each step, you can

rest easy, knowing that your plan development is disciplined and orderly.

Using the PROP framework doesn't guarantee that you will always fulfill your plan, that's for sure. But it greatly increases your chances.

WIN FAST ACTION STEPS

- Pick a goal that you've been thinking about for ages, but for some reason have procrastinated on.
- Give yourself ten minutes to go through the four components of PROP. (You can always repeat them more thoroughly later if necessary.)
- Take action on the very first step of your newly designed path.

DOUBLE YOUR CHARISMA WITHIN A WEEK

Most people think that charisma is innate.
That you either have it or you don't.

They believe that people who exude the kind of magnetic charm that is highly attractive to those around them are just lucky, or born with it.

I think the opposite. I think charisma can be developed and that it can be done so quite easily—if you follow a certain procedure.

I'm confident that charisma has a structure and that it is threefold.

- Charismatic people are very passionate—about their work and virtually any subject they are discussing.

Think about anybody you know who is charismatic. They are really into what they are talking about. They have passionate opinions, even an intensity about certain issues. They are fully engaged in the discussion. You don't see charismatic people being ambivalent. They have one button in their personality and that button is ON. By their sheer commitment to what's under discussion, they are a magnetic force, whereas those around them are sending out weaker energy signals by comparison.

• Charismatic people exude great certainty.

When do charismatic people give out a vibe of being undecided about what they are talking about? *Very rarely.* They have a point of view and express it with gusto. They are confident of their opinions, to the point of dogmatism. Now, they don't browbeat people, they usually keep the vibe fun and on the light side, but nevertheless charismatic people almost always have deeper belief in what they are saying than others.

By the way, they can still be wrong as often as anyone else! But you'd never know it by the confidence with which they argue their point. I am reminded of the autobiography of Donny Deutsch, one of the most successful ad men of the last fifty years. He titled his book, *Often Wrong, Never in Doubt.*

• Charismatic people are sincerely interested in others.

They really lean into whatever conversation they are having. They are genuinely, truly, madly, deeply interested in what you or I have to say. They are not one of those people who always have half an eye looking around the room, searching for someone else who may be more interesting. You get their full gaze and mind.

That doesn't just make whoever they are talking with feel good, their full focus also lifts the quality of their input into the conversation—enabling them to say wiser words, give funnier responses and ask more engaging questions. As they say: "To be more interesting just be more interested."

- Passion, certainty and interest. These are the elements to a hugely charismatic person.

Can you start being more like this? Damn right you can. No unusual talent or aptitude is required. You can press the accelerator on all three in your life anytime you want to.

And it's worth doing. Charismatic people may not be any smarter than others, but they sure get an easier ride in life.

WIN FAST ACTION STEPS

- The next three times you have significant conversations with people, focus on communicating with passion, certainty and great interest in what the others are saying.

- Observe their reactions. Observe how you feel.

- After each experience, determine if you were more charismatic than usual. If so, commit to giving out these three energies in conversations with others from now on.

HAVE A GENUINE PHILOSOPHY OF EXCELLENCE

When I am coaching executives or entrepreneurs, there are two kinds of performance improvement I work on.

First, immediate tactics that can get them better results fast. Second, long-term mental frameworks that can improve every arena of their life.

Having a genuine philosophy of excellence falls into the latter category.

I have found that almost everybody can quickly take their life to an uncommonly high level if they just commit (or in some cases recommit) to doing everything excellently and demanding excellence from those around them.

If we try to carry out every single thing to a very high standard, in a very short period of time our whole life changes for the better.

The reality is that many of us have become a bit lazy. Our average performance is usually good enough for those around us, so if we are not careful, it becomes our normal level of delivery. This situation is particularly prevalent with highly intelligent or very experienced people whom I mentor—they

can get away with performing at half speed, because their half speed is as good as many other people's three-quarter or full speed.

It's a fool's victory, though, as over time anyone performing at an average pace is slowly overtaken by people who do things at an uncommonly high level.

You see, the excellent don't just get better results, they get noticed much more, too. These two advantages then combine to take them to the top, while the mediocre are left behind. Importantly, the rate that this happens is so slow and barely noticeable that by the time the person realizes they've been left sitting on the shoulder of the highway of success, it can be hard to catch up.

By simply switching your daily intent from getting things done to wowing people with excellence, you step your performance up a level. You get far better results, people respond and notice, your reputation soars and you start to feel invigorated and excited by your work and life again.

Curiously, very few people seek to do things excellently, so when you rise to this plane of performance, you actually have very little competition. As they say, "It's never crowded along the extra mile."

Now, you may be thinking, "Well, Siimon, you want us to perform with excellence, but you also tell us to work quickly. How on earth can we do both?"

The answer is to work with excellence, *in the time you allocate to the task*. It is a way of living that is not necessarily time-based, it is standards-based. It's about aspiring to a high level as you seek to work as efficiently as possible. They are not mutually exclusive, as anyone who has ever watched a video of Picasso painting a masterpiece in minutes can testify.

Yes, time spent on a task is important, but bringing a commitment to your own excellence often matters more. It can change your world.

WIN FAST ACTION STEPS

- Get a piece of paper and split it into two columns.
- At the top of the left column, write "Work excellence," and on the right column put "Personal excellence."
- In each column write down at least seven things you could do to establish true excellence in that area.
- Pick the top three in each category and institute them within the next week.

SET UP POSITIVE MENTAL TRIGGERS AROUND YOU

*Does your environment lift you up or
keep you down?*

Does it inspire you to become a more magnificent person, or just continue as you are?

It's absolutely vital that you design an immediate environment that supports you in being an outstanding performer, because over time, humans are influenced by their environment.

When I talk about improving your environment in this context, I'm not suggesting that you need to make it more fancy or expensive, I'm saying that you should create mental triggers all around you that remind you of both how great you are and how much greater you need to become.

What do I mean by "mental triggers"?

I'm referring to pictures, words and objects that inspire you and remind you of what you've already achieved and still seek to achieve.

Here are some examples of good mental triggers:

Pictures of you giving a speech or leading your team or family. Degrees or awards you have won. Photos of the type of home you aspire to own, or of your body when you were really fit. Drawings that your kids have created or objects that remind you of the people who are at the heart of your life, for whom you are doing all this work. Pictures of noble historical figures or people who have a character that you'd like to emulate—anyone from Gandhi to Lady Gaga; whoever inspires you is acceptable.

It could be signs with key words on them that are meaningful only to you, or quotes about life, love or success.

There's no right or wrong mental trigger, it's really what works for you to remind you of what you've done, what you're aiming to do or who you wish to become.

It can be hard to maintain lofty aspirations when the going gets tough and victory seems a million miles away. But if you choose the right mental triggers and place them around you, just by looking at them you will be reawakened to who you are or can soon transform into.

The next time you are with a highly successful person in their home or office, take a look around you. I'm certain that you'll notice that they've set up several mental triggers to support them to continue to aim for great things.

Your surroundings shouldn't just be pleasant, they should be inspiring. It's easy and inexpensive to create mental triggers, and they can make an extraordinary difference in how you feel and act.

WIN FAST ACTION STEPS

- Look around the environment in which you spend most of your day.

- Does it invigorate you? Do you see items that increase your confidence about both your abilities and your future?

- What else could you add to your environment so that you are constantly boosted, encouraged and inspired?

TO SUCCEED, INCREASE CONTROL OF YOUR ENVIRONMENT

Here's a remarkable concept to think about.

How much success you achieve in your life is directly correlated with how much control you have.

Different parts of your life require different types of control, but control still remains crucial in every area.

Professionally, it's all about gaining control of your time and your environment.

Low performers don't exert control over their day. They don't plan it well and they respond to others too much—their emails, calls, requests for meetings, lengthy discussions and demands for work. But look at any super successful person at work and you'll see that they have taken control of all those areas.

With happiness, control is also necessary.

A nationwide study by the University of Michigan has shown that people who feel in control of what's happening in their life are usually much happier than those who don't feel that sense of autonomy. Indeed, a commonly reported feeling by many people with depression is that their circumstances appear beyond their control.

Then there's control of your thinking.

If you can control what you think about so that most of the time your outlook is positive and constructive, you will achieve far better results. Numerous studies have shown that in almost every profession, optimistic people are more successful.

With health and diet, once again it is all about control. The self-control to go to the gym when you don't feel like it. Or to skip dessert when you're out at a lovely restaurant.

Control, control, control.

Why this concept is so important is that once you see the connection between your level of control and your success, you can start focusing on increasing the degree of control you exert in any given situation—and your results will quickly improve. You will see the world in a whole different way.

Unhappy? Look for what you can take control of. Unsuccessful? What areas of your work can you step up and increase your control of?

At your work, look at controlling your time spent on worthwhile activities versus trivial ones. Control the time you spend with clients. Control the time you are in meetings. Control the time you leave work.

To increase your happiness, look for ways you can take control of any situations you are not happy with. Either seek to actively change your circumstances to increase your control of them, or exit those situations altogether. Control your habitual negative thought patterns with more supportive, positive ones.

In every area, aim to increase your control of everything you can.

Of course, there's a chance that those around you will deride you as being a control freak. But you will end up achieving loads more than people who let others control them.

Control is something most people do not think enough about. But it's central to almost everything you want to achieve.

WIN FAST ACTION STEPS

- Write down three aspects of your life that you are not totally happy with.
- Now search for areas within each where you are short on control. You will always find them.
- Take the two most serious of these areas, then brainstorm ways for you to take back control of them.

MAGNIFY YOUR FEAR OF LOSS

There are two ways you can motivate yourself to take a lot of action towards fulfilling your goals.

The first and most common way is to think about how wonderful it would actually be to make that money, buy that house, meet that life partner, vacation in that destination, etc.

This is a very common method for good reason: it works. When you flood your mind with visions of you experiencing the pleasures of reaching your goals, it energizes you to work harder to make them a delicious reality.

But there's another way you can motivate yourself that is not nearly so pleasant, but has been found to be much more effective. In fact, research about this very method helped economist, psychologist and author Daniel Kahneman win the Nobel Prize. Kahneman is a world-renowned expert in behavioral economics, which studies the effects of psychological, cultural and social factors on the economic decisions we make.

Now get this. Kahneman and his research team discovered that most people are much more motivated by the thought of losing something rather than gaining something.

How much more powerful are our feelings about potentially losing something? More than twice as powerful—2.25 times to be precise.

That's very valuable data for any ambitious person. It means that if you start dwelling on what you could lose if you don't reach your goals, you will be much more driven to act than if you only focus on the delightful upsides of achieving them.

So if you really want to succeed, you need to get very clear about all the bad things that could happen if you fail.

I suggest making a list of them all. What could go wrong in your life if you didn't reach this goal? How bad would you feel? Would you be embarrassed? What kind of disasters might occur? Write these potential calamities down and really attach yourself emotionally to them. (Not to the point where you despair, of course, but enough so that you get really fired up about it.)

Do this right and your motivation level will soar.

The ultimate formula for ultra motivation is to use both sides of the coin. First think deeply about all the bad things that could happen if you fail, then think about all the fabulous things that will happen when you succeed. This will really get you moving.

It's important to think about both sides regularly. If you just do it once, you'll get an initial jolt of motivation that will soon wane. You must keep the awful ramifications of loss and the bliss of success at the top of your mind, as you work on achieving your goals week after week.

Yes, it's not the most enjoyable thing to frequently think about what could go wrong in your life if you fail. But it sure gets you up in the morning, raring to win.

WIN FAST ACTION STEPS

- Take a long, hard look at your goals and dreams. What would happen if you totally failed to achieve them? Write down every bad thing that could occur. Don't hold back. Feel the pain.

- Sum up these negative outcomes on a single page. Make the title at the top "What my life will be like if I don't achieve my goals."

- Now do the same in the positive. Title it: "What will happen if I do achieve my goals."

- Read both every morning before you start work.

REMEMBER THE THEORY OF WEAK LINKS

How do you succeed in today's world?

Focus, effort, learning, optimism, persistence, and self-discipline are key. Everyone knows about these as concepts, and a small percentage of people actually work on these attributes.

But there is one other way to succeed in life that virtually nobody knows about, but is equally important.

Weak link associates.

In 1969, a sociologist by the name of Mark Granovetter realized an extraordinary thing. That people you have met but don't know very well are much more useful to you than your close friends or associates.

The kind of people Granovetter was talking about are people you used to work with ages ago, old school friends you've lost touch with, people you only occasionally stay in touch with, people from totally different backgrounds and geographic areas, people you've just met but don't know well, etc.

Your social weak ties.

His theory was that your close friends and associates usually move in very similar social circles to you so they are

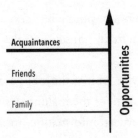

less likely to be able to connect you to people who could help you whom you don't already know.

Whereas the people you barely stay in touch with, those on the outer edges of your contact base, are much more likely to move in entirely different social and business circles. Therefore there's a much greater chance that they could introduce you to valuable people who you never knew existed.

This is a very important concept, as most of us know that we should do more networking to increase the chance of creating opportunities, but almost everyone focuses on developing deeper ties with people we already know quite well.

Granovetter's theory of weak links (which has been developed by other sociologists over the last 40 years) suggests we should regularly reach out to our weakest social links to keep—and even develop—the connection for a time in the future when we may need their assistance.

Now this is a totally different way of thinking to traditional networking, yet entirely logical, in my view.

I have to admit though, that the whole concept of deliberately networking with people for my own personal benefit makes me a little uncomfortable. I much prefer staying in touch with people just because I like them.

But when it comes to purely business connections, I can certainly see the merit in consciously developing the weak connections.

Because when you look at most of your successes in life, you didn't actually achieve them alone. Usually other people helped you—with crucial information, introductions, advice or references.

So it makes enormous sense to cultivate more social connections, and having strong weak links is a very clever way to do it.

WIN FAST ACTION STEPS

- Think of ten people who you only slightly know who could be useful connections.
- Reach out to them in some way. Send them an interesting article, meet them for a coffee, invite them to a group lunch, text them or call up and just say hi.
- When next at a business event or out socially, attempt to speak to at least five people you barely know or have never met.

JUDGE YOURSELF BY YOUR EFFORT, NOT YOUR RESULTS

There is a popular school of thought that the only thing that counts is your results. If you win big or achieve the goal you're going for then this should be all that matters.

I beg to differ. While clearly getting a good result is terrific and a fine accomplishment, it is not the highest level of achievement.

The real champions of life evaluate their success on how hard they tried, not just whether they won.

It's a subtle difference, but in the world of elite performance it's a very important one.

Let's explore it.

It's quite possible for instance, that you could achieve a goal without really trying.

Yes, you accomplished the goal, but you could have achieved much, much more if you'd put your heart and soul into the job.

By purely focusing on reaching a particular result you actually lowered your potential level of achievement.

To all your friends and associates, it looked like a phenomenal victory. But you would know deep inside that you could have accomplished so much more if you had given it everything you've got. You functioned well below your real potential.

The truly great person is going for the very best they can deliver. Don't get me wrong, they certainly set goals and chase them with massive focus and determination, but they also strive to succeed beyond them.

I think it's a superior way to live, because in the end you are not actually in control of whether you win in life. You are only in control of the effort you put in.

Another competitor may have better equipment, more money behind them, better social connections or have been given knowledge that was hidden from you that enabled them to be victorious. So if you base your happiness and self-esteem purely on coming first, you create unnecessary pain in your life.

Now I'm not saying that we shouldn't go hard for the result we desire. We should do precisely that. All I'm emphasizing is that when it comes down to it, the result is beyond your control. So focus on what you can control—your effort.

As one of the greatest basketball coaches of all time, John Wooden, taught his players, it's effort and attitude in the present moment that are the two most important things to focus on. As he put it: "Don't measure yourself by what you've accomplished, but by what you should have accomplished with your ability."

WIN FAST ACTION STEPS

- Spend some time pondering these two questions:
  1. What would you rate the effort you put in each day, on a scale of one to ten?
  2. How can you get it to a ten?

HAVE A LIFE PURPOSE

*I have some questions for you. Simple questions
with truly profound implications. Ready?
Okay, let's go.*

Why are you on this planet?

What do you hope to get out of your experience on Earth?

What is your life's purpose?

Truly amazingly, almost nobody can clearly answer each of these questions. There's a good reason for that. They don't actually *have* a life purpose.

Think about how crazy that sounds. There are more than 7 billion people on this planet, and the vast majority cannot give you a clear, well-thought-through answer to one of the most important questions there is: what their primary aim is in being here.

Now I'm not talking about why we are here metaphysically or spiritually—your belief in God or Mother Nature and your role in the Universe at a cosmic level is between you and the Creator.

I'm being practical. What is the core aim that is driving your life each and every day?

For the simple fact is this. If you don't have a clear reason for what you're doing and how you are living, then you can't possibly be performing at the highest level available to you.

There's no right or wrong answer to this question, either.

Upon reflection, you may say your life purpose is to be happy. Or to enjoy every day. Or to evolve yourself to the highest level possible. It could be to experience God or reach enlightenment. Maybe your primary life purpose is to be a great mom or dad. To uplift others. To help the less fortunate. Or make ten million dollars and give it all to charity. Who knows, perhaps your life purpose is to visit every country in the world, or become number one in your field. Or to create a solid amount of wealth for your children.

You may well have several life purposes.

There's no judgment here; anything that feels right and inspiring to you can constitute a fine life purpose.

But you should have one, because if you don't, you will inevitably be less effective each day. To some extent, rudderless. As the legendary motivational speaker Zig Ziglar expressed it, "You will become a wandering generality rather than a meaningful specific."

Even worse, with no clearly defined life purpose, there's a real danger that you will get to the end of your life and realize that you didn't spend your time as wisely or joyfully as you could have. Which is a devastating conclusion to reach.

But when you have a clear life purpose, you become much more motivated to take action. You see more clearly and make decisions more rapidly. You consciously work to enlarge what really matters to you, because you have determined what that is and you're aware the great clock is ticking. You spend less time on the trivial and more time on the priceless.

Once you decide your life purpose, you will live a wiser and more beautiful life.

WIN FAST ACTION STEPS

- Set aside some quality quiet time alone to ask yourself this most crucial question.
- Imagine yourself near the end of your life and think about how you would want to have lived.
- Write down your thoughts.
- Wait a few days, then return to your notes, think deeply once more, then choose your life purpose.

BE INFLEXIBLE, WITH FLEXIBILITY

There's one sure sign of someone who is going to fail in life.

They change their minds all the time.

You know the type. They start off with huge enthusiasm towards a goal, but when you see them again three months later, they are working on something totally different.

They suffer from the classic bright shiny objects syndrome—whenever they see something alluring, they can't resist giving it a try.

This kind of person looks down so many rabbit holes that they end up getting nowhere. And catch very few rabbits.

The reality is, unsuccessful people usually take a long time to make important decisions and change their minds often. Successful people tend to make important decisions more quickly and stick with them.

In 1970, Harvard University political scientist Dr Edward Banfield set out to determine whether there was one main reason why people rose to a higher socioeconomic level in life. After years of research he concluded that there was.

Successful people have "long-term time perspective."

They think in years or decades, rather than weeks or months. They may not be as talented as some of their competitors, but they persist in the pursuit of their goals longer than them. Slowly iterating, quietly improving, until they end up achieving something truly magnificent.

You need to think seriously long term if you want to reach a higher plane of success in life. Even when your "friends" advise you to give up, even when your competitors are running rings around you, do not be discouraged and doggedly keep going.

But in my view, that's only half of the winning formula.

In tandem with being inflexible about what your goal actually is, you also need to be extremely flexible in the approach you take to achieve it.

Too many people think that there is honor in endlessly banging their heads against the wall, doing exactly the same thing again and again even if it's not working, in the name of persistence.

The opposite is the case. Yes, certainly they should persist, but they should also continually vary their approach until they find one that works. By being inflexible about their goal but being hyper flexible with their approach, they will eventually end up discovering something that works and guarantees victory.

Inflexible but also flexible. This is the key to success.

WIN FAST ACTION STEPS

- Think about a goal you're working on right now.
- Ask yourself, are you trying enough different ways and means of achieving it, or just doing the same old thing?
- How could you vary your approach? Who else could help you? How could you attack the problem from three new angles?

BLOCK OUT DAILY
THINKING TIME

As you can probably tell, I'm pretty big
on efficiency and productivity.

It never ceases to amaze me how much good stuff people who are highly efficient can get done versus the average person. It's no exaggeration to say that in one week the most efficient people can often get ten times more done of value than normal folks. (Think about their increased productivity over a ten- or twenty-year period, and the difference is staggering.)

But as big as I am on doing a lot of tasks quickly, there is the danger of being too obsessed with doing; we can be so busy that we forget about an equally important activity.

Thinking.

A lack of quality thinking time is a huge problem these days. People rush around at breakneck speed, desperately trying to get things done, but forgetting that their success in life will depend as much on the quality of their thinking as the amount of action they take.

And to think efficiently, we need to stop whatever we're doing and take substantial amounts of time to just think

Think

Use a pen when thinking

about our situation and the best way forward, before moving forward.

Thinking about new ways to do work. New ways to handle tricky workmates or family members. Thinking about different ideas that could transform your industry. Thinking about a myriad of things that are occurring in our lives.

It is so tempting to just keep working all day long, because taking constant action gives us the feeling of progress. As Albert Einstein noted, "People love chopping wood. In this activity one immediately sees results."

But action is not necessarily progress at all. It can often be the opposite of progress, if we have chosen non-optimal actions. After all, you can spend your whole life climbing a ladder, only to find with dismay that it's leaning against the wrong wall.

We need time to think—every week—if we are to make the most of opportunities in all areas of our life.

Here's the solution.

Block out 20 minutes thinking time each work day in your calendar. That is less than 5 percent of the average person's workday—virtually nothing. But I assure you that if you spend 20 minutes each day thinking, really thinking, about your circumstances and how to improve them, you will experience an absolute revolution in your results.

Because your competitors are spending a fraction of their workday thinking deeply. Well-nigh everyone is totally caught up in the maelstrom of movement, the avalanche of action, rather than doing the sometimes hard and confronting work of thinking.

What specifically should you do during your daily thinking block?

Just write down questions and answer them.

How could I improve my company? What am I sensing about this situation? Who can help me with this? What am I doing that I should stop doing? That sort of thing.

Simple questions, but questions that have the potential to transform your entire life, if you take the time to think about them.

WIN FAST ACTION STEPS

- Set up your daily thinking time in your calendar.
- Think of five broad topics that can act as springboards for each thinking session.
- If you are in a thinking session and have trouble coming up with anything worthwhile, focus on what you are currently doing well in your life and what you could improve.

USE ZBT TO QUICKLY TRANSFORM YOUR LIFE

Do you feel as if you're stuck in the slow lane and you are not sure how to get out of it?

Are you a little confused or unsure about the next steps to take on your journey to success?

ZBT can really help you.

I've found practicing ZBT every few months can enable you to almost instantly clarify what you should stop doing, what company you should work in, what projects are worth your time and even who you should hang around with.

ZBT stands for Zero-Based Thinking, and it's a mental filter or technique that can be applied equally in your professional and personal life with lightning-quick results.

When you practice ZBT, you look at all the major areas of your work and life and ask yourself just one question:

Knowing what I know now, would I still have done this?

If the answer is "No," then look to get out of it, as soon as possible.

Here's why Zero-Based Thinking is so powerful. So often in life we behave as if we are trapped in numerous situations when in reality we are not. As a result of us forgetting that we can eject ourselves from almost any situation if we really want to, we sometimes spend years (or decades!) trying to make the most of something that we shouldn't even be involved with in the first place.

We forget that in many cases the correct strategy is to exit, pronto.

Now I know, I know, sometimes it's not that easy. Especially when finances or feelings are involved. But the beauty of applying ZBT everywhere every three to four months is that one of two things happens.

You either realize that you need to get out of a deal, a company, a relationship or some other entanglement. Or you realize that even though you cannot get out of it, it is time for some serious changes or conversations to take place.

At its heart, using ZBT is a wake-up call to not settling for mediocrity in your life. It shines a light on what either needs to be eliminated or comprehensively overhauled.

ZBT can be universally applied. It's just as effective to determine whether or not you should stay working at your current company as it is in clarifying if you should continue to hang out with an old group of friends.

So many of us believe we are trapped in various situations, but that is rarely the case. We are freer than we imagine, provided we identify what is no longer working and have the courage to act on it.

Eject or correct.

And in general, those who live by Zero-Based Thinking lean toward the first option.

WIN FAST ACTION STEPS

- Look at your work. Apply ZBT.
- Look at your romantic relationship. Apply ZBT.
- Look at your friendships, the town you live in, your philosophies, your investments, your home and the objects within it. Apply ZBT to them all.

USE MY THREE SUCCESS-PROTECTION QUESTIONS

Achieving lasting success can be hard.

First you have to make it. Then you have to avoid losing it.

The annals of history are filled with people who made it all the way to the top, only to make one bad move and lose it all.

Fortunately, this is unlikely to happen to you if you remember to utilize my Three Success-Protection Questions.

Every month, put a note in your calendar to spend a few minutes contemplating the following questions, and you will triple the chances of keeping your success once you've obtained it.

Here they are:

1. **What do I currently assume is true, that may not be?**
   This is such a powerful question to regularly ask
   yourself. Because when you think about it, many of
   the major problems you experience stem directly
   from you making an incorrect assumption at an earlier
   point. Even right now, there are important things you

think are true in your life or business, that are not. Within each error is both potential opportunity and calamity.

2. **What could possibly go wrong?**
   Study the most successful people in the world and you'll see they are often pondering what disasters could potentially destroy them.

   Bill Gates reportedly had a picture in his office of Henry Ford, the father of the modern automobile industry, to remind him that the mighty can be left behind. One of Silicon Valley's greatest leaders, Andy Grove, wrote a book called *Only the Paranoid Survive*. Frank Lowy, co-founder with John Saunders of gargantuan Australian shopping-center empire Westfield, was asked how his family maintains its success. He answered, "Because we have a siege mentality." Great people who stay great are always looking for what could go wrong.

3. **What could I do if things went wrong?**
   Awareness of possible danger is half the battle; the other half is having a plan of action in case that danger becomes a reality. You need to think through and develop emergency contingencies for every potential failure or weak point in your empire that you can think of. Prepare well in advance.

When bad things happen, speed of response is paramount, before things deteriorate. All massive fires start with just a tiny initial spark.

These Three Success-Protection Questions are extremely valuable. Be sure to ask them when the skies in your life are the bluest and the seas are at their most tranquil.

WIN FAST ACTION STEPS

- Write down the three most important areas of your business or personal life.
- Ask yourself the Three Success-Protection Questions for each of them, and carefully write down the answers.
- Put a note in your calendar to review the answers at regular intervals throughout the year.

DON'T JUST HAVE *DOING* GOALS, HAVE *BEING* GOALS

Lots of ambitious people have goals. Typically, these are goals centered around improving three areas of life: wealth, health and relationships.

(Have a think about your own main goals now and they will almost certainly fall into those categories).

Generally, though, these goals are what I call Doing Goals—they are all about doing stuff that leads to externally measured achievement (e.g., make a certain amount of money or purchase a particular car, house or item of clothing).

Of course, there's nothing wrong with such outwardly centered achievement goals. In fact, having a strong set of them is really important if you wish to progress in the material world.

But for the greatest likelihood of success, you need to balance these Doing Goals with a set of Being Goals—goals specifically aimed at improving how you are inside as a person.

The fact is, unless you develop your character internally, it will always be difficult to attain major external goals. To achieve more, you must first become more. But most people don't think that way. They incessantly strive for external, material goals but do virtually no work on the only vehicle that can take them there: themselves.

With that in mind, here's a life-changing exercise to try.

For each wealth, health or relationship goal you have, write down one to three character traits that you would need to develop in order to reach that goal.

Will you need more persistence, patience or confidence? Will you need to develop more focus, calm or raw desire?

Take a moment to think about these Being Goals. For how you are inside is always eventually reflected in your outside results. Pear seeds can never become apples.

Once you have clarity about how your character needs to change to enable the achievement of your external goals, it's time to work on these Being Goals each day.

One of the founding fathers of the United States of America, Benjamin Franklin, had an excellent method for doing this. He wrote a list of 13 Virtues, character traits he knew he needed to develop if he were to become someone special. He then focused for seven days in a row on improving just one of the virtues. For example, one week he focused on being frugal, another week he centered his efforts on being humble, and so on.

By concentrating on just one area, he quickly made meaningful progress. He also doubled his chances of success by keeping meticulous records of how he performed each week. There are very few people on the planet who would bother to do this, and so it's no surprise that very few people in history have achieved as much as Ben Franklin.

Develop your Being Goals along with your Doing Goals. It will rapidly accelerate your progress in any field you care about.

WIN FAST ACTION STEPS

- After you have written down your Being Goals, put them somewhere you will see them each morning.
  - Commit to improving on these aspects of your character daily.
- If you have a bad day, don't see it as a failure, just accept that it is normal, and recommit.

APPLY THE PLUS ONE METHOD EVERYWHERE

When you set out to reach a really big goal, the path to fulfilling it can quickly become pretty disheartening.

The road seems so long, the steps seem so many, the obstacles so overwhelming, it's quite understandable that after a while your motivation can weaken and thoughts of giving up soon crowd your mind.

At times like this, it pays to remember that every substantial accomplishment was achieved by hundreds (or often thousands) of tiny steps forward, rather than a handful of huge leaps.

That beautiful building you admire each time you walk past it? It took hundreds of thousands of tiny actions to build it. That beautiful long-term relationship two lovers enjoy? It's only because of millions of small actions they took that made it so. That incredibly inspiring company that everyone admires? That's the result of billions of small steps taken by the founders and employees.

The tiny is the fabric of the great.

With this in mind, it's easy to see why the Plus One method is such a formidable addition to an ambitious person's arsenal.

Here it is, in a nutshell.

Every time you feel like progress on your goal is too hard, ask yourself, "What's one thing I could do right now to move this forward?"

It could be something as simple as phoning someone. Or sending one email. Or online research on how to do something. Or spending a few minutes planning. Or reaching out to a friend for help. Or studying a competitor who's further down the line of progress than you.

Usually the Plus One is something small. Something quick. Something easy to make happen.

But as soon as you do that little Plus One activity, an interesting thing will happen.

Because you've made some progress, you'll feel more energized and motivated to reach the goal.

What do you do then? Just look for your next plus one, and the next, until pretty soon you've created major momentum towards your goal.

Truly, one of the most important things I've ever learned about success is this: ordinary performers wait until they feel good before they act. Top performers act until they feel good.

That's the brilliance of the Plus One method. If you keep doing it, you'll not only make loads of progress, you'll also begin to feel fantastic.

So please, memorize the Plus One question and make it a habit to ask it several times a day. You'll come to appreciate that there are in fact no great achievements, just groups of tiny achievements living together.

WIN FAST ACTION STEPS

- First, write down the Plus One question and memorize it. You'll be using it daily going forward.

- In the next 24 hours, aim to ask the question five times and take action on the answers immediately.

- Observe how it creates momentum and lifts your spirits.

CONCLUSION

TAKING YOUR LIFE TO THE NEXT LEVEL

Congratulations, now you have the Win Fast formula.
A series of unusual, proven and powerful
ways to massively increase your level of success,
quickly and efficiently.

This stuff works. I use many of these techniques when I coach executives, entrepreneurs and ambitious people all over the world. They routinely report that the methods in this book have helped them monumentally to increase their income, well-being and happiness.

Now it's your turn. You've got the toolkit for change; now you have to use it consistently. The world is full of people who read books and then put them on the shelf, the concepts never to be utilized in their life. They came so close to designing a life of richness and fulfillment, only to falter at the point of action.

But not you. You are different from the masses. You're committed to transformation, not just information. That's how you ended up choosing this book and reading it all the way through. You are going to take the systems in *Win Fast* and use them to better your life in all four of the areas of work, personal life, health and mindset.

Here are some tips for making the most of the Win Fast system.

IDENTIFY THE CRUCIAL FEW.

Remember the 64/4 Rule? It applies with this book, too. Out of the 80 methods in *Win Fast*, there will be a handful that will have made an extra impact on you. These are the ones where as soon as you read them you realized they were exactly what you needed to transform your life or work.

Perhaps one directly addressed how to overcome an obstacle that you've struggled with for years. Or maybe you tried another and found that you enjoyed almost instant improvements. I am sure there are some that you just know that you'll be using again and again through your life. Please create a list of these.

KEEP THEM FRONT AND CENTER IN YOUR LIFE.

I have conducted a lot of experiments in my own life in order to work out how I can increase the chances of putting effective life-improvement techniques into action. I've found that when I set up reminders I can make remarkable change happen, and when I don't keep the concepts at the top of my mind I tend to forget them.

That's why I strongly advise that you stick up your "crucial few" short list of concepts somewhere you'll see them often. It could be on a Post-it Note on your desk or up on a wall in your bathroom—or even on a card in your purse or wallet.

The more you see them, the more the concepts will be in your mind—and the more they are in your mind, the more you will act on them. When you read these techniques each day, you set the stage for momentous life improvements to happen.

PERSIST AND REFINE.

As you know, there are some pretty radical ideas in the Win Fast system. You may think some even border on weird! I know from my own experience that they are all extremely effective, but in some cases you may need to try them a few times to experience their full force.

Please keep this in mind when you initially struggle with a method. If it appealed to you originally, then it is almost certainly worthwhile persisting with, to see if you can get it to work.

For example, some of the mind techniques I present often take a few tries before they become natural for many people, but they are exceedingly valuable tools for life enhancement and are well worth using.

Likewise when it comes to refining the techniques. As you

use them in your own life, you may have the urge to adapt them a little to fit your own needs. That's absolutely fine; in fact I recommend it. Tailor them as you see fit. The important thing is that they work for you and that you are comfortable with them, so if that means you alter them to fit your needs then that's totally appropriate.

SHARE THEM.

There are two advantages to sharing some of your favorite Win Fast techniques with people who matter to you.

The first is that it's a well-known fact among professional educators that when you have to teach a concept to others, it considerably deepens your own understanding of it. If you really want to grasp anything at a higher level, teach it to someone.

The second reason is that the more successful and evolved the people around you are, the better your own life will be. And, of course, theirs as well. Imagine if your closest friends and loved ones were all using this system to better their lives and increase their happiness. That would exponentially uplift each of your lives.

BELIEVE IN YOUR ABILITY TO CHANGE.

My final tip is to always keep at the forefront of your mind that whatever level you are now at, you can rise higher.

The core foundation of change is the conviction that change is possible.

Once you truly believe deep inside that you can become better, smarter, faster, richer or happier, you have won half the battle.

That kind of self-belief is a choice that you make. I urge you to make it right now.

From this moment onwards take the position that you deserve to have an even greater life, that you're capable of doing so and that you're committed to rising to a new stratosphere of excellence.

With this book you now possess an extraordinary armory of techniques that if you apply consistently, can greatly improve almost any aspect of your life. All that's needed now is the will to do so and the belief that you can.

Go for it.

THE TOP THREE METHODS TO HANDLE YOUR SPECIFIC CHALLENGES

This book is all about getting results fast. So in this section I've grouped together the top three techniques that I recommend when you have a specific issue or situation that you need to solve.

Whenever you're challenged in a big way, come back to this page and try the three techniques that I recommend for your particular problem. Do all three methods immediately, to help you win faster.

WHEN YOU ARE UNCLEAR OF WHICH DIRECTION TO GO

- Create great plans in ten minutes
- Use the Bezos decision-making system
- Get super clear about what you want

WHEN YOU ARE FEELING
GENERALLY UNMOTIVATED

- Set up positive mental triggers around you
- Be your own motivation coach
- Create a set of five life rules

WHEN YOU NEED A BURST OF CONFIDENCE

- Apply the Plus One method everywhere
- Create a three-person superhero
- Follow my Four-Step Productivity System

WHEN YOU NEED TO INCREASE
YOUR ENERGY

- Do One-Minute Workouts
- Use sleep as a weapon
- Work under full-spectrum lighting

WHEN YOU WANT TO IMPROVE
YOUR RELATIONSHIPS

- Double your charisma within a week
- Don't just have *doing* goals, have *being* goals
- Have a clear finish time

WHEN YOU HAVE TO BECOME MORE PRODUCTIVE

- Use a timer all day
- Follow the 80 Percent Good principle
- Live by the 64/4 Rule

WHEN YOU WANT TO MAKE MORE MONEY

- Block out daily thinking time
- Get an accountability partner
- Have a genuine philosophy of excellence

WHEN YOU FEEL REALLY DISORGANIZED

- Have a weekly admin day
- Make your desk like the Sahara Desert
- Follow the Two-Minute Rule

WHEN YOU'RE GETTING CRUSHED BY STRESS

- Follow a morning ritual
- Think game, not war
- Use the release breath to keep your stress low

WHEN YOU WANT TO WORK FEWER HOURS

- Practice the Two-Hour Day
- Rush the unimportant
- Do your most important tasks first

WHEN YOU DESIRE TO TURN YOUR LIFE AROUND

- Aim to be in the top 10 percent of your field
- Use the science of luck
- Have a learning goal each quarter

WHEN YOU ARE SEEKING GREATER HAPPINESS

- Change your mood with your posture
- Clear your mind each evening
- Make the most important choice in the world

FREE GIFTS ONLY FOR READERS

I really appreciate you reading this book.

As my way of saying thanks, I've created some free gifts and bonuses only for my readers.

If you like the *Win Fast* book, you should really like these presents, as they extend a lot of the thinking in my book.

Just visit www.siimonreynolds.com/gifts to download them:

- A video of me talking about my top five techniques from the book
- A checklist of ways to quickly improve your life
- A short paper on powerful ways to grow your business
- An audio interview of me talking about how to increase your chances of success

ACKNOWLEDGMENTS

This book is the result of an enormous amount of work by a team of highly talented and remarkably committed people.

Thanks go to my superb agent Julie Gibbs. Your style and expertise are very much valued.

To the stellar crew at Penguin Random House: publisher Nikki Christer, my editor Clive Hebard, designer Adam Laszczuk and proofreader Lauren Finger. Thanks for your patience, creativity and wisdom. It's been fantastic working with you.

I'm deeply appreciative to my loyal and long-serving assistant, Tania Sukiennik, for her support over all these years.

To my business partners Brian Sher, Andrew Miles and Paul Hooley, thank you for all your help and for all those nights eating ribs.

A big shout-out to the Eisman family: Sylvia, Peter, Jacqui and Daniel. Your love, care and jokes are greatly appreciated.

To my brother, Guy, and sister, Harriett. Thank you so much for being there for me, in good times and not so good.

Finally, to my wonderful wife, Kathryn, and my daughters, Capri and Monet. You are my inspiration, the center of my life and my great loves, forever.

WORKING WITH SIIMON

If you got value from this book, there are several ways you can work with Siimon.

KEYNOTE SPEECHES AND WORKSHOPS

Siimon speaks on high performance, leadership, productivity, sales and marketing, innovation and business growth.

His energizing and inspiring keynotes blend cutting-edge research with unforgettable stories to make him one of the most highly ranked speakers at any conference or company training event.

ONLINE BUSINESS COURSES

Siimon has created several practical online courses on how to quickly and systematically grow your business. He teaches powerful techniques to increase your company's income and rapidly scale your enterprise.

PRIVATE CONSULTING

Siimon mentors entrepreneurs, CEOs and highly ambitious people from all over the world on maximizing their personal and business achievements. Consulting is usually via Skype or one-day intensives.

For details of any of these, visit siimonreynolds.com